KT-488-292

THE PRIVATE EYE ANNUAL 2006

EDITED BY IAN HISLOP

"Look – it's the fabled Lost World"

Published in Great Britain by
Private Eye Productions Ltd
6 Carlisle Street, London W1D 5BN

© 2006 Pressdram Ltd
ISBN 1 901784 43 6
Designed by Bridget Tisdall
Printed and bound by
Butler and Tanner Ltd, Frome and London
2 4 6 8 10 9 7 5 3 1

THE PRIVATE EYE ANNUAL 2006

EDITED BY IAN HISLOP

"This is absolutely disgraceful!
When was this room last cleaned!?!"

Since she was 3 years old, the Queen has owned no fewer than 7,310 corgis, and she can remember all their names.

The Queen's nickname for Prince Philip is "Roger".

 The Queen has never eaten a prune in her life.

The Queen owns the 78th largest stamp collection in the world.

 The Queen's shoe size is 3½.

The Queen's favourite "Carry On" film is "Carry On Up The Khyber".

 The Queen's favourite dish is spaghetti bolognese.

The Queen is distantly related by marriage to the late comedian Spike Milligan.

 The Queen can complete the Daily Telegraph Quick Crossword in less than two hours.

The Queen has her own personal dustman.

The Queen's mobile phone has the ring tone "God Save The Queen", a birthday present from her grandson Prince Harry.

The Queen owns the world's largest emerald, the "Star of Balti", given to her great-grandmother Queen Victoria by the Akond of Swatch.

The Queen and Prince Philip are ardent DIY enthusiasts, and once decorated the spare bedroom at Sandringham during a weekend in 1961.

The Queen owns a pet tortoise, believed to be 264 years old, which she calls "the Duke of Windsor" after her uncle.

When the Queen was introduced to singer Engelbert Humperdinck at a command performance in 1974, she mistook him for the actor Sir Laurence Olivier.

The Queen's favourite TV programme is The Sweeney, which she never misses.

During the Second World War the Queen smoked a pipe when she was in the ATS.

When she was only four years old, the Queen had violin lessons from Sir Edward Elgar, the well-known composer.

The Queen is an Arsenal season ticket holder.

EIGHTY THINGS YOU DIDN'T KNOW ABOUT HER MAJESTY THE QUEEN

(one for each year of her glorious reign)

Of the 28 prime ministers who have served under her, her favourite was Stanley Baldwin.

The Queen has visited Australia 97 times, but has never been to the Pacific islands of Satnav and Vanunu, even though she is their Head of State.

The Queen's favourite flower is the hydrangea.

The Queen is allergic to pepper.

The Queen has used 23,481 separate pairs of scissors to cut over 900,000 miles of ribbon at opening ceremonies.

The Queen has a lifetime subscription to the New Scientist magazine.

The Queen is a gifted mimic and can do all the characters from the popular TV series Little Britain.

The Queen took up pole-dancing when she was living in Malta in the early days of her marriage

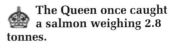

The Queen once took a ride on the London Underground between Leicester Square and Piccadilly Circus.

The Queen's Coronation Coach cannot go backwards.

The Queen once caught a salmon weighing 2.8 tonnes.

The Queen never allows the name "Peregrine Worsthorne" to be mentioned in her presence. No one knows why.

According to a law of 1154, which has never been repealed, all stoats belong to the Queen and killing a stoat is still a capital offence. The last felon to be punished in this way was Peter Stoatherd, who was hung at Wapping in 1538.

The Queen's jodhpurs have been traditionally made for her in the Indian city of Jodhpur.

The Queen has recently become an avid devotee of reflexology which she believes cured her sciatica.

When the Queen was introduced to the famous writer Rudyard Kipling, she mistook him for Engelbert Humperdinck, the popular singer.

As Head of the Church of England, the Queen has the power to imprison any churchman up to the rank of Archbishop.

The Queen's favourite TV programme is "Dad's Army", and when she once met its star, Arthur Lowe, she mistook him for Rudyard Kipling.

The Queen's favourite dish is prunes, which she likes to eat with pepper.

The Queen's pet name for Prince Philip is "Engelbert".

The Queen has never been to a Premiership football match.

The Queen is allergic to tortoises amd will not allow one to be kept at any of her homes.

The one Commonwealth country the Queen has never visited is Australia.

The Royal Coach can only travel backwards.

 The Queen has never been to the toilet.

(That's enough things you didn't know about the Queen. Ed.)

'HELP ME!'

– DROWNING MAN'S PLEA

by Our Man In Washington **Bill Oxi**

TODAY I saw with my own eyes one of the most tragic spectacles I ever hope to witness.

Standing alone on the roof of what was once his home, as a flood of toxic filth rose ever higher towards his isolated refuge, a solitary white male survivor shouted, "Please save me! I don't know what to do. I've lost everything."

When our helicopter got near enough for me to speak to him, the inarticulate Texan sobbed out to me his pathetic story.

"They tell me my name is George Dubya Bush," he stammered. "Everything seemed to be going along just fine and dandy until this hurricane came along. The next thing I knew, I was up to my neck in effluents. And my world just fell apart."

While we spoke, he was joined on the rooftop by several friends and neighbours, who were also desperately trying to avoid the rising tide of dead bodies and costly insurance premiums that threatened to submerge them.

They gave their names as Condy 'Gumbo' Rice, Donny 'Jamaican' Rumsfeld and Dick 'Halliburton' Cheney.

Most tragic of all was the sight of Mr Bush's aged mother rowing a small yacht around Washington in the hope of drawing attention to her son's plight.

"It's all right for them poor black folks. They got nothing to lose but their lives. But who's gonna save my boy? Nobody, that's who."

CITY THREATENED BY NEW FLOOD

by Our Entire Staff **Phil City**

THE CITY of New Orleans was yesterday submerged under a tidal wave of journalists and TV crews from all over the world, asking people how they felt to be drowning, starving etc. and whether they thought George Bush was to blame.

Fortunately by sundown the flood had disappeared as quickly as it had arrived, when all the journalists went back to their hotels to watch pictures of themselves interviewing people on what it felt like to be drowning etc.

This is clearly the work of al-Quatrina

NEW ORLEANS

"Woke up this mornin'
Someone had looted ma guitar..."

ROBERT THOMPSON

Who's this Katrina Fund?

I sure hope she's cute

Bush Clinton
Katrina Fund

NEW NEW ORLEANS

"This area here will be the ghetto..."

🏛 **The Delphi Telegraph** 2 Obols

Atlantis – It Must Never Happen Again

BY OUR FLOOD STAFF AMANDA PLATO

As the world woke up to the scarcely believable disaster which has engulfed the great city of Atlantis, one message came out loud and clear from all sides of the political spectrum – it must never happen again.

For centuries, oracles had warned that building a city several cubits below sea-level was a disaster waiting to happen.

Shock

The noted hydrological expert Professor Cassandra of Troy University repeatedly went on record prophesying that sooner or later the city of Atlantis would be flooded, bringing death and destruction to all its inhabitants.

However, the prophetess's cries of woe were ignored, as the citizens of the famous "party city" continued to eat, drink and make music with-out any thought for tomorrow.

The few survivors of the worst natural catastrophe the ancient world has known were quick last night to blame the Atlantis state authorities for failing to build up the sea walls which could have saved the city from inundation.

"Instead of looking after our homeland security," shouted one enraged Atlantean from his rooftop, "all our troops have been sent to Mesopotamia.

"No wonder there is no one here to save us," he added, as his house finally sank beneath the waves.

Britons Feared Lost In Flood Disaster

Two ancient Britons, Sid and Doris Flintstone, were among those who (cont. p. 94)

The New Inclusive St Paul's
How It Will Look
As approved by The National Lottery

LOUIS HELLMAN

Beano Boris analyses the new problems posed by the escalation of the insurgency in Iraq

CRIPES. I mean, blimey. Did you see those pictures of the chaps getting out of that tank, all covered in flames? Crikey. That's not very nice, is it?

I mean, don't get me wrong. I was one of the first to start cheering when our lads went in. I even went to Iraq, I think. Big place. Lots of sand. Chaps with towels on their heads. Anyway, it all seemed tickety-boo then. At least, that is what I was told by Brigadier 'Squiffy' Squiffington, who would know because, not only is he in charge out there, what's more, he was at school with me.

But, no sooner was my back turned than, golly, the whole place is swarming with swivel-eyed malcontents, chucking milk bottles full of petrol all over the nearest tank.

Phew! That's not exactly the point, is it? I mean, didn't we go in there to help Johnny Iraqi enjoy a bit of freedom, democracy and all that stuff? And now he's trying to set us on fire.

I blame that blighter Blair for getting us into this mess in the first place, and anyone who supported him. Whoops! Cripes! Blimey! etc.

© The Daily Beanograph.

The Daily Telegraph

September 30th 1843

NEW DISABLED STATUE 'A DISGRACE'

by Our Man In Trafalgar Square **W.F. Deedes**

The new statue erected in Trafalgar Square has attracted a storm of protest, with objectors claiming that its portrayal of a disabled figure is "sensationalist" and "in poor taste".

The statue, designed by controversial artist William Railton, depicts a one-armed man who is partially blind.

"Railton is just trying to shock people and make headlines," said one critic. "His statue does the disabled no favours at all and ruins the look of the whole square."

Asked for a reaction, the subject of the statue, Admiral Horatio Nelson, was unavailable for comment on account of being dead.

ON OTHER PAGES

Will His Highness The Prince of Wales ever become King? page 2

Is the fetching Miss Lillie Langtry secretly addicted to laudanum? page 3

The Mousetrap – tickets available page 94

POLLY FILLER

SO the male medical establishment has decided in its infinite (or should that be 'infantile'?) wisdom that women should *not* put off having children until they are older. Oh, pur-lease!!! Obviously useless men don't want women to have careers because then we won't have time to look after them as they sit around all day watching Extreme Pro-Celebrity Sudoku with Natasha Kaplinsky and A.A. Gill. So what could be better in the great male conspiracy against us working women than to have "wifey" (or "partnery"!) having her sprogs young and staying at home rather than establishing herself as, say, a top columnist and best-selling author of *Easy Mummy! – Further Collected Dispatches From The Front Line Of Modern Motherhood* (Johnson and Pearson, £12.99).

WELL, let me ask this simple question on behalf of so-called having-it-all mums everywhere: If women are obliged to have children in their early Twenties then who on earth are we going to get to be our nannies?

It's hard enough to get decent girls as it is – we've just said goodbye to Chi Po from China who seemed to think that 35p a week wasn't enough to supplement her board and keep, even when she put Simon's underpants in the DVD player rather than the washing machine! Honestly! What do they teach these girls in rural villages nowadays?

But imagine if Chi Po and all her ilk were *having* children instead of looking after ours very badly. Where would we be then?

You see... *men*, they never think things through!!
© Polly Filler.

"He's being held under the Prevention of Heroism Act"

BERNIE

7

KATE MOSS ADDICTION LATEST

by Our Fashion Staff **Cocaine Chanel**

THERE were mounting fears last night about the future of the British press, when it became clear that it has become hopelessly addicted to Kate Moss.

What started as an occasional experiment has now become a full-blown habit with journalists "doing hundreds of lines" a day. In fact, some papers cannot get through a single page without an enormous "hit" of Kate Moss.

Said one observer, "It's a tragic spectacle. Editors go into the toilet looking tired and depressed and then come out minutes later excitedly demanding features about Kate and crackhead Pete."

Gets Up Your Nose

He continued, "The trouble about this addiction is that you lose all sense of reality – you forget that there is a world out there – and all you think about is where you're going to buy your next 'fix' of what they call 'Katie'."

Snorts Pages

He concluded, "The worst thing is that it's so easy nowadays. You buy it cheap, cut it up, and lay it out in the Mirror or possibly the Sunday Mirror."

MOSS DRAMA LATEST

What are you going to do now?

Coke, crack, whatever

SUPERMODELS

KERBER

Kate Moss goes down to the Police Station....

GIVE ME "CRIMINAL" DARLING, ...THAT'S NICE, NOW GIVE ME 'WHACKED OUT ON DRUGS' ...THAT'S LOVELY DARLING...

CLIK CLIK CLIK

325 10 981

GLENDA SLAGG

THEY CALL HER HURRICANE GLENDA – THERE'S NO ESCAPE!

■ **THREE CHEERS** for Kate Moss!?! So she sniffs coke, takes crack and holds amazing orgies in top hotels! So what? She's a party girl!?! She likes a bit of fun, for gawd's sake, after a hard day on the catwalk. What do you expect her to do, Mr Noozman?!? Sit at home with a pot noodle, watching Corrie?!? You gotta be joking!?! I say this – Cokehead Kate has got the courage to stand up and then fall down!?!?

■ KATE MOSS!?! What a disgrace!?! Listen, love, you're not just a model!?! You're a role-model!? Geddit?! What sort of a message are you sending out to the kids, with your sniffin' and a-whiffin', your snortin' and cavortin'?!? You should be ashamed of yourself. I'll tell you what, love. Here's a tip from Auntie Glenda – instead of going out a-cokin' and a-pokin', why don't you stay at home with a pot noodle and watch Corrie?!?

■ **POOR LITTLE** Kate Moss!?! Just because she's been out enjoying herself, the fashion house bosses are queuing up to dump her. Our cuddly Kate has made the high street labels billions, with her waif-like figure and her drop-dead looks!?! Oi, you, Mr Chanel, Mr Burberry and Mr H&M!?! Give Katie her job back. And why not throw in a hefty pay-rise as well, so she can afford more drugs!?!??!!

■ HATS OFF to Mr Chanel, Mr Burberry and Mr H&M?!?! At last the fashion industry is cleaning up its act and sending crackhead Kate a-packin' and a-sackin'!?! It's high time this dope-crazed dolly was made the "new face of the dole queue"!?! Geddit?!?

■ SO JORDAN's got married!!!? Who cares??!? What's she ever done to warrant newspapers going on and on and on about her!!!?! Jordan's carriage, Jordan's dress, Jordan's boobs, Jordan's everything else!?!! Jordan!?! Jordan?!! Jordan!! I'm sick of just writing her name?!!? We're not interested Mr Noosman, so write about something else!!?!?

■ WHAT'S happened to us??! The nation that gave us Lord Nelson and Sir Francis Drake has nothing better to do than sit a-dribblin' and a-droolin' over pix of Jordan and Andre when there are loads of other people we've never heard of getting married too!!!? Jodie Kidd, Kate Garraway, Tom Parker Bowles. Celebrities???!? Don't make me laugh!!! These people are about as famous as my hamster – and you don't see pictures of him in Hello! magazine every time he gets married??!?

■ CRIKEY!!!? What type of world do we live in when I'm reduced to writing about my hamster getting married!!?! Ok, so he can run around in a wheel faster than most people – but do people really want to read about him in a national newspaper!!!? We must be stark, staring mad!!??! *(You're fired. Ed.)*

Fashion Week Toilets

ME AND MY SPOON

THIS WEEK

KATE MOSS

Do spoons play an important part in your life as one of Britain's top models?

You'll have to see my lawyer.

NEXT WEEK: *Kate Moss – Me And My Moss.*

Love Is Blind

by top romantic novelist DAME SYLVIE KRIN

THE STORY SO FAR: The newly-unattached Minister for Pensions seeks solace for his broken heart in the fashionable West End nighterie 'Jezebels'.

Now read on...

"**W**HAT are you having, mate?" The suave Australian barman in the t-shirt emblazoned with the club's logo shouted above the throbbing music that was the hallmark of Mayfair's most fashionable discotheque.

This was not the old David's scene at all. A far cry indeed from the back-to-back houses of Sheffield of his childhood with the outside latrine where his Nan used to have a bath full of coal. *(Is this right? Ed.)*

No, this was the new David. The suave, sophisticated man (and dog) about town, perfectly at ease with the aristocratic coterie of Sir Max Burberry's drink and dancing venue for the moneyed beautiful people of the night. Their braying voices wafted across the room, mingled with the sounds of the club's trendy anthem, Chris de Burgh's 'Lady In Bed'.

"I said, what are you having, mate?" The debonair drinks server from Down Under repeated his question, puncturing David's wistful reverie.

"A pint of Boddington's and a bowl of water for the dog," he ordered hurriedly.

"Strewth, mate! That's no way to talk about the ladies in this joint. Although, between you and me, cobber, you are pretty much on the money."

Shane gave the former cabinet minister a conspiratorial wink and then jerked a thumb at a nearby table full of elderly former debutantes drinking Bacardi Breezers and discussing school fees.

David listened with wonder as the fashionable voices pierced the smoke and the disco din.

"And Rupert did terribly well in his GCSEs..." "My dealer comes round on a bike as if he were delivering pizza, ha ha ha..." "Who's that dancing with Araminta? Isn't it that ghastly Greek chap who writes in the Spectator?..." "...Oh my God, have you seen the scruffy, bearded chap at the bar? How did he get in here?"

David bristled and took a sip of beer.

"Don't take any notice," soothed a soft voice, arriving suddenly at his shoulder, and David could smell the delicate, musky aroma of 'Parfum de Floozie' by Duchamps.

Delicate fingers touched his hand. "Haven't I seen you somewhere before? Your face looks very familiar."

Once again, David swelled with pride at all he had achieved in life and all he had become.

"You probably saw me on the Andrew Marr on Sunday show, talking about pensions reform. I'm often on television, you know."

His new companion, a stunning blonde girl in her late twenties, moved closer to him, flushed with excitement as she realised she was in the presence of the man who would one day determine at what age she would be able to retire from her job at the Estate Agents.

"You're David Blunkett!" she gasped.

"The very same," he said, imagining he was at least as suave as the rest of the nightclub's legendary clientele. There was Sir Andrew Neil, showing off his latest vest and baseball cap to an exotic companion. There was Sir David Frost falling asleep in a corner over a glass of Rio Tinto. But it was *he*, David Blunkett, who was the centre of attention...

"I'm Gilly Northern," she cooed, "and I'm the assistant regional manager of Callard & Bowser Properties. We do short-term lets, long leases, freehold... you're not looking for anything are you?"

The question resonated in David's mind as he removed the paper umbrella that the barman had thoughtfully put in his glass of ale.

Was he looking for anything? Was he semi-detached? Might he need an extension? As if to echo his thoughts, the strains of Dodo's classic single 'Life To Rent' filled the dancefloor...

"**E**xcuse me, sir," a gruff voice intruded on the intimate tête-à-tête at the bar, "I must ask you to leave."

The dark-suited bouncer towered menacingly above the lovestruck former Labour leader of Sheffield Council.

'What do you mean?" he stammered. "Aren't dogs allowed?"

"The dog's fine. But there's a no beards rule here. Sir Mark is particularly insistent on it. He doesn't want people thinking Jezebel's is full of old gits trying to pick up blonde totty half their age..."

The next thing David knew, he was out in the cold night air, sitting on the hard pavement of Berkeley Square.

Somewhere a church clock struck two and a nightingale sang its eternal love-lorn refrain. But what was that? Something wet and warm nuzzling against his cheek... Was it his faithful four-legged friend once again? Or could it possibly be...

(Find out in the next instalment of 'Love Is Blind' unless Mr Blunkett gets an injunction and all further episodes are cancelled)

© Sylvie Krin 2005.

BLAIR EXIT STRATEGY

LORD BRAGG names the 10 books that changed the world

❶ The London Telephone Directory (2005)

Although this is not strictly a book, it is highly readable and includes many influential names from the worlds of literature, science and plumbing.

❷ The Boden Catalogue (1998).

Although this is not strictly a book, this informative and entertaining guide to men's fashion in the late 1990s gives a vivid snapshot of how we were in that formative decade.

❸ The Highway Code (1952).

Although this is not strictly a book, this slim volume codified the etiquette of driving for a whole generation, and influenced millions of motorists.

❹ The Carol Vorderman Book of Sudoku (also available on CD-ROM).

Although this is not strictly a book, this anthology of classic Sudoku puzzles compiled by one of the most distinguished mathematicians of her age was viewed as making a greater contribution to improving mental health among the elderly than anything the pharmaceutical industry had to offer.

❺ Lord Birt's McBraggart Lecture To The Edinburgh Festival Of The Televisual Arts (2005).

Although this is not strictly a book, or indeed in any sense worth reading, it is worthy of mention as a reflection of the collapse of literacy and intelligence in the Britain of the early 21st century.

❻ Sex Among The Daffodils (1975) by Melvyn Bragg.

Although this is not strictly a book, this brilliant novel by myself, about a Wordsworth-loving Cumbrian bank manager who seduces a barmaid on the banks of Derwentwater, is *(cont. p. 94)*

(cont. p. 94)

THE DAILY TELEGRAPH

aren't i marr-vellous?

Mr Drivel
Notebook

hi there, readers, it's me again, mr drivel, the only guinea pig in the world to have his own column in the daily telegraph... haven't i done well for myself? and guess what my subject is for today, as per usual, it's a sad little creature with funny ears whom nobody cares about... yes, andrew marr... now i know most of you would like me to write about something serious but i can't because i'm contracted to the bbc and they won't let mr drivel comment on anything that might be remotely interesting... sorry to disappoint you but i can tell you one thing... i may be only a guinea pig but i get paid a lot more than a guinea for this *(You're not fired. Ed)*

"That's typical of you, Keats – conspicuous consumption"

NEW DVDs

DOWNFALL

Powerful and moving re-creation of the last days of the crazed dictator Adolf Blair, as his dreams of world domination crash in flames around him.

Becoming more manic by the day, we see him sending more and more young men to the front line to try and win a hopeless war.

Accompanied only by his devoted mistress, Eva Booth, and his hated propaganda chief Josef Campbels, he eventually realises that the game is up – committing suicide by handing over the reins of power to his long-time companion, Gordon von Braun.

'A searing insight into the heart of evil'
– The Berliner Guardian

TURNER PRIZE FOR MODERN ARSE

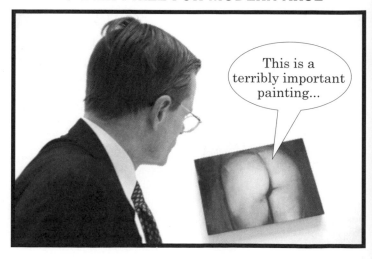

This is a terribly important painting...

POETRY CORNER

Lines on the retirement of Richie Benaud, Australian cricketer and commentator

So. Farewell
Then Richie
Benaud.

You have
Retired – 74
Not out.

"Good morning,
Everyone. It's a
Lovely day
Here at Lord's."

That was your
Catchphrase.

Unless of
Course you
Were at the
Oval.

And it was
Raining.

L.B.W. Thribb (17½)

In Memoriam Mary Wimbush: actress and three-time star of *The Archers*

So. Farewell
Then Mary Wimbush,
Long-running voice in
The Archers.

I am not a
Regular listener
Myself
But Keith's mum tells
Me that you were
Elsie Cratchet in the
1950s, then Lady
Bonham-Strawberry
In the 1970s.
And, more recently,
Mrs Ludmilla
Starborgling,
Mother of
Jasper.

All together now –
Dum-di dum-di dum-di-
Dum. Dum-di-dum-
Di-da-da.

E.J. Pargeter-Thribb

PS: I gather that you / were once the live-in partner / of my fellow bard, Louis MacNeice. / Some poets have all / the luck.

MODERN NURSERY RHYMES

Dr Foster went to Gloucester,
Young and idealistic.
He left with stress
From NHS targets and
statistics.

Who killed Cock Robin?
"I," said the Rook,
"He gave me a funny look."

If you go down in the woods
today,
You'd better not go alone.
The woods are full of kids in
hoods
Who'll steal your mobile
phone.
(from 'Tony Blair's Picnic')

In Memoriam Julio Iglesias Senior, aged 90

So. Farewell then
Julio Iglesias Senior
Father of Julio
Iglesias Junior
And grandfather of
Enrique Iglesias.

You were best known
For your amorous proclivities
In old age
And also of course for being
The father of
Julio Iglesias
Junior and
Grandfather of
Enriquez (cont. verse 94)

Enrique Julio Thribbesias
(aged 97½)

In Memoriam Radio Four's 'UK Theme Tune'

So. Farewell
Then the UK
Theme by the late
Fritz Spiegl.

All over the country,
For 30 years, listeners
To Radio Four
Have woken up to
This medley
Of British folk tunes.

Normally I would give
My readers an
Impression of
How it goes
(See my many tributes to
The Magnificent Seven).

However, I do not know
How it goes, since
I do not get up
At 5.30
In the
Morning.

In Memoriam Mr Gene Pitney, Dixons the High Street electrical retailer, and 'Davina', the BBC1 mid-week chat show hosted by Ms Davina McCall.

So. Farewell then
Gene Pitney, Dixons and
Davina.

You will all be
Missed.

Except for
Davina.

E. J. Thribb
(17½ Hours From Tulsa)

11

YE DAILY TELEGRAPH
September 1785

Is This Man Too Young To Lead The Tory Party?

by William Deedes

He's the upstart new kid on the block. The 'boy wonder' from the privileged background who wants to be Conservative leader at the tender age of 24. But is it too soon for this precious political talent to take on the top job?

Surely we would be better advised to choose somebody older, with more experience of government and with more popular appeal than this Oxbridge wonderboy who has come from nowhere.

That is why we say vote for Pitt the Elder who (cont. p. 94)

CAMERON REFUSES TO DISCUSS 'CONTROVERSIAL PAST'

by Our Leadership Correspondent **Simon Spliffer**

LAST NIGHT top Tory leadership hopeful David Cameron again refused to be drawn into discussing events which he said "all happened a long time ago".

When asked by Andrew Marr "Were you at Eton?", Mr Cameron merely smiled and replied, "Like many others I had a normal educational experience."

When pressed by Marr to admit that this involved "top hats, tails, fancy waistcoats and fags", Cameron was evasive.

Weed

"Look, it's time to move on. What I did or didn't do at school has no bearing on my ability to take drugs (*surely 'lead the party'? Ed*).

"You heard me, stranger. I said ponchos are like so totally last year"

BEANO BORIS – ONLY IN THE EYE

Cripes! I'm Backing My Friend David To Be Tory Leader!

by **Beano Boris Johnson**

BLIMEY! Just look at the list of candidates and you'll see what I mean. All rum 'uns bar my old chum Spliffy Cameron!!

There's clapped-out Clarke, Dullard Davis, Phoney Fox and Rubbish Rifkind!! Crikey!! What a bunch of losers!

Not only can none of them string two words together, but they didn't even go to Eton!! Blimey!

And what about Mrs Spliffy, eh? Phwoarr! She's a bit of a corker, what?! Memo to Boris: Must invite her to the Beano Lunch, nudge, nudge, and make sure that Bounder Blunkett and Randy Rod Liddle aren't there! I saw her first chaps, so clear orf!

© *The Daily Beanograph.*

HEFFER JOINS THE EYE!

Irascible, irritating, unreadable

NOW THAT the candidates for the Tory leadership have shown their hand, those of us who for a long time have been calling for a fundamental reappraisal of Conservative values can feel fully vindicated.

My own choice, which I have no doubt the party will in due time endorse, is for a young, radical, Tory moderniser – ie, Lady Thatcher, who still embodies the *(cont'd. 1894)*

ME AND MY SPOON

THIS WEEK

DAVID CAMERON

What is your vision for spoons?

I think spoons should be attractive, compassionate, relevant and modern. I think they should be well-balanced and improve the quality of life not just for the few, but for the many. Ask not what a spoon can do for you, but what you can do with a spoon.

You yourself come from a privileged background. Does that affect your attitude to spoons?

No, not at all. I think we've moved beyond the old obsession with class – what sort of spoon you eat soup with and that sort of thing.

Could you elaborate a little for our readers on that point?

Well, I like spoons to embrace the best of the traditional past and the exciting design of the future, say a carved wooden handle with the other end made out of plastic or possibly stainless steel – but don't get me wrong, I'm not going to dictate to people what sort of spoons they should use. I'm not Nanny, you know!

Some people say that actually you were born with a silver spoon in your mouth and that this will count against you.

Hey look, guys, I'm in favour of classless spoons and my wife Cherie thinks the same. I'm all spoons to all men. It's what I call the Third Spoon...

Have you ever used a spoon for drug-taking purposes?

How come you don't ask anyone else this question? Why don't you ask me if anything amusing has ever happened to me in connection with a spoon? Then I can show what a human, rounded, funny kind of Tory I am.

Alright then – has anything amusing ever happened to you in connection with a spoon?

No.

NEXT WEEK: *Jon Snow 'Me And My Snow'.*

Who Are They – The Cameron Set That Everyone Calls 'The Camikazes'?

(Surely 'Macaroons'? Ed.)

David 'Dave' Cameron, 27, Eton-educated, PR high-flyer for Croydon TV (producers of 'Good Morning, Croydon', 'Good Evening, Croydon' and 'Good Night, Croydon').

Samantha 'Sam' Cameron (née Fox), 25, gorgeous, pouting, ex-page 3 girl. Daughter of Scunthorpe baronet Sir Edward Fox, chairman of Fox's Glacier Mints, she now runs the swish Bond Street stationery shop Posh Post-Its.

Basil Brush, 35, high-flying 'TV fox' and leading light of influential Tory dining club, the 'Boom-Booms'.

George O'Borne, 25, high-flying shadow spokesman for paperclips, son of the carpet magnate Sir Francis Underlay.

Michael 'Go Go' Gove, 21, high-flying former Times columnist, now MP for Notting Hill South, Gove provides the "intellectual backbone" for the Cameroons.

Tarquin de Vere Cameron, 41, high-flying second cousin of Dave Cameron (and fifth cousin once-removed of Sam Fox). "Tarqui the Rotter", as he is known, works for Sotheby's in the Oriental Ceramics Department, coming in at 10.30am clutching a cappuccino from Pret A Manger and saying, "Cripes, bit of a heavy night last night".

(That's enough people you've never heard of. Ed.)

FRANCE TO JOIN EU?

by Our Brussels Staff **Lunchtime O'Barroso**

THERE were moves last night to allow one of the largest countries in Europe, France, to become a full member of the European Union, despite earlier concern over its refusal to accept the EU's constitution and the fact that the country is full of Muslims.

Said a Brussels spokesman, "Our problem with France is that it consistently fails to comply with EU regulations, it demands massive subsidies for its backward peasant agriculture and, historically, they have an appalling human rights record.

"Frankly," said the spokesman, "they are culturally so different from the rest of us that I cannot see negotiations for their admission to the club ever succeeding."

ON OTHER PAGES: Austria's bid to join human race 'unlikely to succeed' **94**

"Forget it, Bell – no one's going to want a mobile telephone that takes photos and plays music"

GLENDA SLAGG

PRIVATE EYE'S NEW POLITICAL CORRESPONDENT!

■ ARE THE Tories stark raving bonkers!?!? They must be, to drop the one man who could actually win an election against Tony and Gordon!!?!

Ken Clarke, I'm talkin' about, stoopid!?!! The Freddie Flintoff of modern politics and the only man who can hit Tony and Gordon for six!!?! *(You've done this bit. Ed.)* Who says he's too old for the job?! Winston Churchill was over 100 when World War Two broke out. And nobody said he should stay at home by the fire with his slippers and his pension book!?!

Ken is an ordinary bloke, from his trademark cigar right down to his Hush Puppies!?! And he's been around long enough to kick Tony and Gordon into touch any day of the week!?! *(I said you've done this bit. Ed.)*

Yet what did they do?! The future saviour of the Tory Party was shown the door!? Shame on you!!? You deserve to lose!!?

■ THANK GAWD!?! The Tories have shown some sense at last – by giving the heave-ho to Fatso Ken, along with his stinkin' cigar and his has-been Hush Puppies!?!

Talk about the day before yesterday's man!!?! 65?!!? You look more like 165!!!?

Time to go home and sit by the fire with your slippers and your pension book, and listen to your rotten old jazz records.

Fag off, Ken!!?! (Geddit?)

■ GLENDA'S Top 10 Tories: Sorry guys, there's only one!!?! **David Cameron** – mmmmm!?!

TOMORROW: Glenda's 10-point plan for solving Britain's pension crisis.

THE Sun

Friday, October 14, 2005

INSIDE SEX SECRETS OF THE SUDOKU SLAVES p 69

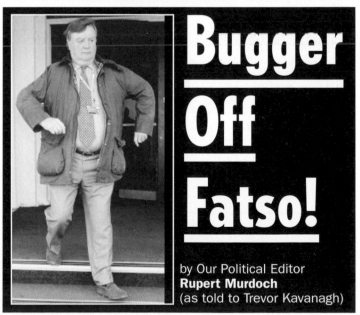

Bugger Off Fatso!

by Our Political Editor **Rupert Murdoch** (as told to Trevor Kavanagh)

OK, so Ken Clarke may have won himself a 10-minute ovation. But then so did Adolf Hitler.

There is no hiding the fact that Fatboy Ken is smoking and drinking himself to death.

And he's keen on Europe. What more need we say?

The Sun says – there is only one man fit to be Tory leader. And that man is Tony Blair! *(Is that right, Rupert?)*

ON OTHER PAGES: Win A Night In Gaol With Tax Rebel Vicar

13

BIRD FLU
Your Questions Answered

Are we all going to die?

Yes and no. On the one hand, the strain of flu virus called BNP 94 is highly contagious and can spread from chicken to human, leading to instant death. But there is no likelihood that this will happen in Britain. Unless it does.

But what would happen if it did happen?

At the moment, all the evidence shows that in its present form, WD40 cannot be transmitted from birds to cattle (or vice versa). If it did, it would create a pandemic which would kill more people than the great Belgian flu outbreak in 1903.

Should we kill all birds before it's too late?

The answer to this one is yes and no. Yes, I'm not sure, and no, I haven't a clue.

© *An expert.*

A Doctor Writes

AS A doctor, I'm often asked, "Doctor, have I got Bird Flu?". The simple answer is "No".

"But, Doctor," the patient continues, "I've got all the symptoms – I'm sweating, shaking and feeling nauseous."

"That's because you've read too many articles about Bird Flu," I reply.

What happens is that the patient buys a newspaper in which there is a large piece saying, 'Bird Flu Killer – Millions Will Die'.

This transmits itself neurologically to the brain where it begins to mutate into panic, hysteria and depression.

The worry is that this condition, or Avianis fluensis apocalyptus as it is known to medical experts, may spread from human to human until we reach a point where the entire population is infected, including myself. My advice is PANIC!!! WE'RE ALL GOING TO DIE!!!

© A. Doctor.

Play All New Bird Flu Sudoku!

1		8	4	9		7		
2					6	9	8	
4		3			7		2	
		6	2	8				9
	5						4	
3				1	4	5		
	1		5			2		3
	3	9	7					8
		7		4	8	6		1

SIMPLY place any number at random into the grid on the left to produce a figure, and if it matches the number we've plucked out of the air and put onto our front page as our prediction as to how many people will die from a Bird Flu pandemic – you're a winner!

"*...And Human Looman went into a complete panic, screaming 'The Bird Flu is coming, the Bird flu is coming'...*"

WHAT YOU CAN BUY AT THE GREAT MAXWELL HOUSE CLEARANCE SALE

● 1 Life Jacket (unused)

The Ronnie Barker Who Knew Me

RONNIE BARKER was very lucky to work with me at the start of his television career. I am sure he would have been the first to admit that he owed his subsequent success to that early lucky break.

© *J. Cleese.*

POETRY CORNER

In Memoriam Ronnie Barker: actor, writer, comedian

So. Farewell
Then
From me.

And so
Farewell then
From him.

E.J. Thribb (17½)

FROST JOINS AL-JAZEERA

Halal, good evening and welcome

Love Is Blind

by DAME SYLVIE KRIN, author of La Dame Aux Camillas, Born To Be Queen, Heir of Sorrows , etc.

THE STORY SO FAR: Suave pensions' supremo David Blunkett has whisked off his new love, Gilly Northern, for a special Romantic Autumn Break Weekend at the palatial Thames-side Ramada Cliveden (£95 for two, breakfast not included, pets welcome).

Now read on...

THE shining orb of the October moon hung in a starlit sky, bathing the famous gardens of Berkshire's most celebrated country house hotel in a silvery sheen.

The rippling waters of the ancient River Thames reflected back its radiance, as two swans glided silently by.

Yes, this was a night for lovers.

And there, on the Nancy Astor Terrace, leaning casually over the 18th-century stone balustrade, their arms lovingly intertwined, were the handsome, debonair former Home Secretary, elegantly dressed in a white tuxedo, and Gilly Northern, the beautiful blonde Assistant Regional Manager of Callard and Bowser Properties.

From inside came the soft strains of the Christopher Silvester Suppertime Sextet playing a medley of hits from the long-running musical Les Miserables.

"Happy, darling?" whispered the love-struck former leader of Sheffield Council into his companion's delicate ear.

"Of course, David," she murmured in reply. "Who wouldn't be? What with the moon, and the stars, and the swans, and this divine music. Which reminds me, I've always wanted to be an opera singer. You don't know anyone, do you...?"

David thought for a moment. Of course he knew someone. It was not for nothing that he was the Secretary of State for Work and Pensions, one of the most powerful members of the government.

"I could have a word with Tessa Jowell," he smiled. "She's the Culture Minister, you know. And a good friend of mine..."

There was a discreet cough at his elbow. It was Weatherspoon, Cliveden's legendary Maître d'Hôtel. "Excuse me, sir, your table for dinner is ready. And, of course, a bottle of our best Tesco champagne is included in the 'Lovebirds Two Nights For The Price Of One' package."

"THESE oysters go down a treat," said the hirsute New Labour high-flier, wiping his neatly-trimmed beard with an immaculate linen serviette, embroidered with the legend *'Property of the Ramada Group – Do Not Remove'*. "Beats fish 'n' chips any day.

"We have so much in common," he went on, "a love of fine food, fine music, fine poetry – and perhaps, who knows, we may discover an even greater bond...?"

"It's a lovely thought," Gilly replied distractedly, "but tell me more about

these influential people you know in the opera business."

As if by some telepathy, Maestro Silvester raised his baton, and his sextet launched into their musical *'Tribute To The Three Tenors'*.

Gilly couldn't resist joining in, as the unforgettable opening bars of Nessun Dorma floated across the polished floor of the Lord Halifax Ballroom.

"What a beautiful voice you have," said David. "Would you like to have my babies?"

Before a startled Gilly could react to David's outburst, the venerable Maître d' appeared beside their table.

"Is everything to your satisfaction, Mr Blunkett?" he enquired.

"It is so far," joked the man once hailed as Britain's most successful education secretary, "but I'm hoping it'll get even better as the night goes on!"

The Maître d', smiling discreetly, refilled the two champagne flutes on the table before him. "If I may say so, sir, it is just like the old days, when this wonderful old house welcomed great statesmen, such as yourself, and the

beautiful young ladies they had met in London."

The aged factotum's eyes lit up, as he remembered the amorous ghosts of yesteryear.

"Ah, yes," he said half to himself, "those were the days. Mr Profumo. Pretty girls. Midnight parties round the swimming pool."

His reminiscence was interrupted by the sound of Gilly's mobile phone playing Mozart's immortal G-Minor Symphony.

"Oh, hullo, darling," she chirped into the phone. "I can't talk now. I'll have to ring you back in a couple of minutes."

"Who was that?" David asked casually, trying to keep the note of suspicion out of his voice.

"Oh, just someone from the office," she replied breezily.

"What? At 11 o'clock on a Saturday night?" David countered, beginning to show a hint of impatience.

"It's a bungalow in Wokingham," she explained hurriedly. "It's just come on the market. Will you excuse me? I'll just go and sort it out..."

"THE bar's closing, sir. Would you like another pint of Boddington's – or has sir perhaps had enough?"

David heard the Maître d's voice as if from a long way away.

"Now that we've agreed that madam is not coming back, I've taken the liberty of transferring you from the Mandy Rice Davies Honeymoon Suite to a single room on the 6th floor. It is a considerable saving for you and your dog.

"Easy does it, sir," he went on, as he guided the forlorn man-of-affairs across the now deserted dance floor towards the lift.

"And, by the way, I've just remembered how it all turned out for that minister I was telling you about – Mr Profumo – and his young ladyfriend.

"He was caught out lying and he had to resign. He ended up doing charity work in the East End. Terribly sad..."

At that moment the band launched into the final number of the evening, and Maestro Silvester himself took the microphone to sing his signature tune, *'When Your Lover Has Gone'*.

Outside in the garden the moon had long since vanished behind the clouds, and the swans had gone their separate ways.

© The Gnome Hellenic Cruise Collection 2005, 'A Voyage Into Romance'.

IS DIANA STILL ALIVE?

By Our Royal Staff **M. Fayed**

SENSATIONAL new evidence has come to light that Princess Diana was not murdered in Paris in 1997 by the Royal Family, as everyone has previously thought, but is still alive and living secretly on the front page of the Daily Express.

Said top Royal expert Mohammed Fayed, who has been investigating the Diana mystery for many years, "I will give you a lot of fugging money if you print this in your fugging paper."

Full story and pictures: 2-94.

FRENCH NATIONAL ANTHEM

Allons enfants de tous les immigrés ♪ 🎵

The Tragic Causes Of The French Riots

HA HA HA... serves them right... they had it coming... don't lecture us about immigration... garlic... onions... cheese-eating surrender monkeys... Feu what a scorcher! Geddit!! Ha ha ha...

© All newspapers...

"I had hoped for something a bit more romantic"

Was Cherie's New Hairstyle A Mistake?

Before

After

YOU DECIDE

0898 7423471

✔ **YES IT WAS** and you hate her

0898 7423472

✔ **YES IT WAS** and Blair should resign at once

PUNCH AND RICHARD AND JUDY

"It's not very exciting – they just sit on the sofa and chat"

Mary Ann Bighead

YOU WILL BE SAD to hear that this is the last column I shall be writing for a while, since I have decided to go on a year-long intellectual voyage round the world with my children. Obviously, this means I have to take them out of school, which is something I would normally disapprove of – as a stern Times columnist.

However, my children Brainella (3) and Intelligencia (7) are so fantastically clever and well-adjusted that they can only benefit from the mind-broadening experience of spending so much time with their very clever parents. Any fear that they might fall behind in their studies is easily dispelled by the fact that their father can teach them astrophysics, biochemistry, neurosurgery and nanotechnology, whilst I can cover the arts – history, geography, English literature, the Classics, philosophy, politics, economics and, of course, languages (French, Spanish, German, Italian, Russian, Serbo-Croat, Classical Persian, Mandarin and Swahili!).

Of course, the main thing that I can teach them as we go round the world becoming cleverer and cleverer is ... MODESTY!

©Mary Ann Bighead, The Times.
Mary Ann Bighead's Diary 'Around The World In 80 Columns' begins tomorrow.

The New Alternative Rocky Horror Remembrance Service

No. 94. To be read in all churches on Sad Face Day (formerly Remembrance Sunday)

Chair *(for it is she)*: Brethren and sistren. We are gathered here to remember that some things are better forgotten – i.e. war. So can we start with a short silence when we try to remember what it is we've forgotten.

(Here there shall be a two-minute silence. Or one-minute silence, if that is sufficient. Or no minutes, if it is so deemed)

The Solemn Pledges

Chair: Do you solemnly commit yourselves to work for a world in which unpleasant conflict of any kind has been totally eliminated in a real sense?

All: We so pledge.

Chair: Do you further commit yourselves to working for the integrated welfare of the wider community, whether by air, land or sea?

All: We so pledge.

Chair: Do you also commit yourselves to developing a drive towards a sustainable racial and equality agenda, with full access for the disabled?

All: Indeedy we do.

Chair: In the name of religious, social and ethnic inclusiveness, we shall now sing that wonderful chorus by Yusuf Islam, from *Hymns Ancient And Muslim*, 'Morning Has Broken'.

Chair: That was nice, wasn't it?

(There shall now follow a suitable reading from the new translation of the Desiderata, *as transcribed from The Holy Teacloth Of Bury St Edmunds)*

Reading

"Go peacefully through the streets and don't do anything I wouldn't do! Enjoy! Be lucky! Bless!"

(At this point the service shall terminate with the playing on a trumpet [or it may be sampled from an electronic keyboard, should the Scouts and Brownies be unable to provide a trumpet or player] of Mr Louis Armstrong's much-loved hymn 'What A Wonderful World'. The congregation may join in with any bits they can remember)

All: ... trees of green ... skies of blue... dum-di-dum... la-la-la... think to myself, what a wonderful world...

(The congregation shall then proceed to the site of the old War Memorial, now the new Tesco extension, to carry out the traditional act of Sunday shopping)

RADICAL PLAN FOR TODDLERS REVEALED

by Our Educational correspondent **Charles Moocow**

THE Government today announced a radical new plan for the education of nought to three year olds called 'childhood'.

"Apparently 'childhood' has been used around the world in a vast number of countries for many thousands of years as a means of educating very small children," said the education secretary Ruth Kelly. "Toddlers who've been allowed to enjoy a 'childhood', which consists of unstructured play and fun, are said to have enjoyed many benefits later in life."

However the Government's 'childhood' proposals were attacked by educationalists who said that they could leave some three year olds with a reading and writing age of three, *(cont. p. 94)*

"Yes, I do mind if we educate him while we conceive him"

DUBYA'S PRAYER TO GOD

Give us this day our daily dead

Introducing

EYE TOAST

FREE with today's Private Eye and every Tuesday – all the latest goings-on in the exciting world of toast.

● **The Russian Toast Billionaires** 3

● **How Toast can make you live longer** 7

● **Madonna on "My First Piece of Toast"** 23

● **Toronto is the toast of Toast** 37

'MORE BOBBIES ON THE BEEB'
demands Police Chief

by Our Broadcasting Staff **Yesminister Alibi-Barmy**

POLICE Chief Sir Ian 'Blair of the Yard' Knacker today appealed to the public to tell him what he should be doing, since he has no idea.

Delivering the BBC's annual Bumblebee Lecture, Sir Ian said: "It is up to the public to tell the police what sort of police service they want, in keeping with the needs of the 21st century."

Stop And Search Me

"The idea that you ring 999 and ask for a bobby to come round and help you because you are being robbed, raped and murdered is very last century.

"What we are looking for from the public is suggestions as to how the police can spend more time on the television.

"As our new slogan has it, 'We want more bobbies on the Beeb'. The message we are getting from the public is that they are reassured by the sight of a friendly policeman on their television, asking them what it is that the police are meant to do."

● *Listen to Sir Ian's speech in full on our new Eye Podcasts!*

"Next left, you idiot, not right! Now we'll probably be late!"

That Honorary Degree Citation from the University of Haifa In Full

SHALOM ET SALUTAMUS DAVIDIUS BLUNKETTUS CELEBRATUM MINISTERIUM BRITTANNIAE PRO LABOR ET PENSIONES APPOINTMENTUM IMPERATORIS ANTONINUS BLAIRUS AD MMV ET QUONDAM DOMUS SECRETARIUS STRINGEMUPPISSIMUS SED UNFORTUNATER LEGOVERUS SCANDALUS MAGNATUS CUM BIMBONA AMERICANA KIMBERLEIA QUINNA ET PATER FILIUS DISPUTATUS QUOQUE PROCURAVIT VISA CELERERRIMA PER NANNIA FILIPINA ET ALTERO SCANDALUM CUM LEGOVERA BIMBINA PEROXIDIA AMICA MAXI CLIFFORDENSIS ET FREQUENTAVIT DISCONE NOCTURNO APPELLATA ANNABELLI ET RECEPIT PECUNIAS IRREGULARIAS EX CONSORTIO DIRIBONUCLEICACIDUS (DNA) CONTRA CODUM MINISTERIUM SED, EHEU, FINALITER DISMISSUS EST EX CABINETO AB IMPERATORE TONIO BLAIRIO (VIDE SUPRA), DUX UNIVERSEA ET OMNES GALACTICORUM, ET RETIRAVIT AD SHEFFIELDUM CUN CANE NIGRO LABRADORENSIS FIDELIUS NOMINE SADIA. GAUDEAMUS ET BONUS RIDDANCIUS AD GARBAGIUM MALUM.

© University of Haifa (formerly Oranges 'R' Us of Jaffa).

THE ARCHERS

What you will hear in the saga that has gripped the nation

(Cow moos in background)

Emma Grundy: Will, I've just been into Ambridge to buy one of those testing kits from DNA Bioscience...

Will Grundy: Oh yes? And...

Emma Grundy: I think you should know that the baby... it's not yours.

Will Grundy: Oh my god! Don't tell me it's Ed's!

Emma Grundy: No...

Will Grundy: Then who?

Emma Grundy: Yes – it's David Blunkett's.

(Dog barks. Silly theme music plays – Dum-dee-dum-dee-dum-dee-dum, dum-dee-dum-di-da-da.)

(Cont. 94kHz)

The New Eye Game Play Siddiki!

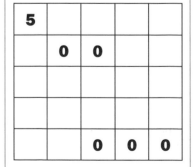

5			
	0	0	
	0	0	0

FILL in the figure you think David Blunkett was going to make from "Businessman" Tariq Siddiki!!

A TRAGEDY OF OUR TIME

The resignation of David Blunkett marks a sad end to a long and distinguished career of public service... humble beginnings... triumph over disability... leader of Sheffield council... extraordinary grasp of detail... won universal respect... key role in Blair project... immense abilities... regrettable intrusion into his private life... lonely divorcé... unfortunate liaison with married woman... understandable lapse... quite rightly brought back into government... questions of judgement remain... "kiss and tell" blonde... dodgy businessmen... more dodgy businessmen... "will you have my babies"... share scam... filling boots... gross breach of ministerial code of conduct... more gross breaches... appalling scoundrel... quite unfit to hold public office... stupid beard... should have been kicked out years ago...

© All newspapers.

Now from the creators of **Janet And John** comes **Tony And Ruth And John** – The Easy-To-Read Education White Paper In Full

Tony wants reform. Ruth wants reform. Tony and Ruth want reform. John doesn't want reform. Tony wants John to be quiet. Ruth wants John to be quiet. Tony and Ruth want John to be quiet. John says, "Fook off yer poncy public-school boogers!"

When you can read this White Paper you can go on to Reading Stage 2 – **Tony blames Ruth for the abject failure of his government to improve educational standards over the last eight years.**

"You're right! It takes something like this to bring the neighbours together and actually talk to each other!"

Last Night's Soaps
WHAT YOU MISSED

South Westenders

(Int: Fashionable home in Battersea. Ross and Rebekah have been out celebrating at a big party. But Ross has found out Rebekah's guilty secret)

Ross: You slag!

Rebekah: Who are you callin' a slag?

Ross: I don't believe I'm hearing this.

Rebekah: Leave it out!

Ross: It's Blunkett, innit? You've been out wiv Dirty Dave ain't ya?

Rebekah: You don't know nuffink. You're just all mouf you are.

Ross: What's your game then?

Rebekah: I'll see who I like, right?

Ross: I don't believe I'm hearing this.

Rebekah: Shut it!

Ross: Don't tell me to shut it!

(Rebekah punches Ross in the face. Cut to the house nextdoor where nice couple Tom and Jenny are getting worried by these violent scenes)

Tom *(on phone)*: Hello, police... I'm terribly sorry about this, but the ghastly couple next door are having a bit of a domestic. She's the editor of some awful tabloid and he's the yobby one from Eastenders. I don't watch it myself, but Jenny does, she's just here, she can tell you all about it.

Policeman: I don't believe I'm hearing this...

(Cut to police station where Rebekah is being bundled into a cell)

Rebekah: You're makin' a big mistake. You don't know who you're dealing wiv. I've got friends in high places.

Policeman: I don't believe I'm hearing this.

Rebekah: Tony, Cherie, Rupert, they're all my mates and your job won't be worth nothing when they find out what you done to me. And I know Max Clifford.

Policeman: Blimey, I'd better let you out then.

(Cut to int. Sun editorial office. Next morning. Rebekah is sitting at desk, clutching head and taking an Alka-Seltzer. Rupert Murdoch enters)

Rupert: Strewth! You're drunk, violent and stupid.

Rebekah: Yes, boss.

Rupert: You're a perfect Sun editor. Have a raise!

Rebekah: I don't believe I'm hearing this!

Rupert: Now let me have a look at those page 3 sheilas. Jeez, look at the melons on this one... you'd need a kangaroo's pouch to get them home...

(Credits and silly theme tune)

Cast In Full

Rebekah Wade...Barbara Windsor
Ross Kemp..............Grant Mitchell
Dirty Dave.............Ricky Tomlinson
Dirty Digger........Barry Humphries

GREAT SUN HEADLINES THAT SOMEHOW FAILED TO BE PRINTED.
NO 94.

IT'S THE 'ED 'ITTER OF THE SUN!

COMING SOON

Blunkett & Gromit
THE CURSE OF THE WERE-DID-IT-GO-WRONG

HILARIOUS comedy from Wallace Blunkett, the crackpot Northern inventor of excuses, and his far more intelligent sidekick, Gromit the dog. Trouble starts when Blunkett falls for posh totty Mrs Kimberly Quinn and makes a fool of himself. Then he does it again and again!

Enjoy Blunkett's loveable catchphrases, including:

● *"We're at it like rabbits!"* ● *"Cracking crumpet, Gromit"*
● *"Can I join the board of your company, Mr Siddiqi?"*

CAST IN FULL

DAVID BLUNKETT ....Peter Sallis
GROMIT ....Sadle
MR SIDDIQI.. Ralph Fiennes
LADY KIMBERLY QUINN .... Helena Bonham-Carter

EYE RATING: FAMILY COMEDY AT ITS SADDEST!

"My God, how embarrassing – mutton dressed as mutton"

Maily Telegraph

Ex-Telegraph proprietor on multi-million pound fraud charge

By Our Media Staff
Phil Job

LORD BLACK of Alcatraz was last night charged with the biggest theft in history having stolen billions and billions of pounds to maintain his lavish lifestyle which included the following incredible items:

● **A fleet of personalised jets (£89bn)**
● **A penthouse on the moon (£173bn)**
● **Napoleon's original toothbrush – as used at the** Battle of Austerlitz (£278bn)
● **The world's most expensive wife (£1233bn)**
● **The world's most terrible newspaper (65p – free on Eurostar)**

Lord Black of Alcatraz was, however, unrepentant. Speaking from his 147-bedroom Toronto hideaway he told reporters, "I am completely innocent. They can send me to St Helena if they like but I will be back. And this time I will win."

Full story: Not in paper due to embarrassment of all concerned.

Conrad Black denies wasting shareholders' money on frivolous items

---

VERY QUICK TELEGRAPH CROSSWORD

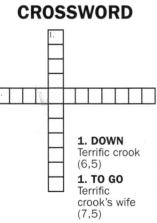

1. DOWN
Terrific crook (6,5)

1. TO GO
Terrific crook's wife (7,5)

Winner becomes new editor.

Sales Of Telegraph Soar To New Low!

FOR the fourth month running Telegraph sales have rocketed down to a record 94 copies. Why don't you join the throng of thousands of readers who are deserting the Telegraph and buying the real Daily Mail instead. (Is this right? Marketing Dept.)

Telegraph editor throws in towel – 'I can't stand it anymore'

By Our Media Staff
Phil Job

MR MARTIN Newboy, the 25-year-old editor of the Maily Telegraph last night suddenly resigned to the amazement of nobody except the men at the Telegraph. Said one marketing man "We had no idea he was the editor. We just told him what to put in. Newboy will be sadly missed but not for long since he is going to be replaced by a computer – just like the crossword compiler."

Full story: Not in paper due to further embarrassment of all concerned.

MATT

"At last, something worth reading in the Maily Telegraph!"

EXCITING NEW MAILY TELEGRAPH POD-CAST!
Download the Best of Simon Heffer's trenchant views on why David Davis should be Tory leader

THE NEW
SUNDAY GNOMEGRAPH
BY EDITOR SARAH STROBES

INTELLIGENT, elegant, classy, relaxed... but enough of me! In today's world few of us have time to read newspapers, or indeed to write them. That's why the new-look *Sunday Gnomegraph* has adopted an innovative "thin" format so that it doesn't contain loads of half-baked frothy articles designed to fill up the pages... like this one! For me, a Sunday newspaper is like a bath bubble, floating in the air, smelling of perfume, with a picture of a woman in her knickers on the front page.

And, just like a bath bubble, it should leave you transformed, fragrant, news-based and waspish.

That's why you'll love our new magazine, "Nutella" – it's creamy, chocolatey and easy to spread on your bread. Not to mention focusing on core news values around the world.

In short, my dream is that the *Sunday Gnomegraph* is like an iPod – full of old rubbish that you don't want to listen to. *(Is this right? Brillo.)*

Sarah Strobes

In this week's Nutella

Pants: In or Out? by Matthew D'Ancona
Shoes: the new socks? by Chris Booker
How to open a tin of soup by Niall Ferguson
Top Ten Hats by Simon Heffer
PLUS **Nothing else**
PLUS **Free DVD of terrible old film that's on Sky this evening anyway.**

STREET CRIES OF OLD LONDON
THE PEERAGE SELLER

Bring out yer dosh!
Bring out yer dosh!

That New 'Are You British?' Test In Full

● **If you want to know the number for directory enquiries, which number do you ring:**
(a) 999; (b) 112; (c) 123; (d) 94949494.

● **Who won the University Boat Race in 1923? Was it:** (a) Oxford; (b) Cambridge; (c) The University of the North Circular (formerly The World of Leather).

● **Is beer sold in:**
(a) gallons;
(b) kilograms; (c) millilitres;
(d) hectares.

● **Does the younger son of a marquess take precedence over the heir to an Irish Baronetcy?**
(a) yes; (b) no; (c) don't know; (d) whatever.

● **Is David Beckham:**
(a) a footballer; (b) a candidate for the Tory leadership; (c) the former secretary of state for work and pensions; (d) the heir to the throne.

● **Who repealed the Corn Laws? Was it:**
(a) John Peel; (b) Emma Peel of the Avengers; (c) Wayne Rooney; (d) the late Thora Hird.

● **Can you spot the odd one out?**
(a) Carry on Doctor; (b) Carry on Nurse; (c) Carry on drawing your social security benefit.

Congratulations: you have scored 0 or under and you are now a British citizen. This makes you a legitimate target to be blown up by a terrorist, and to pay a huge amount of tax, should you decide to work during your stay.

If you do not speak English do not worry you can take this test in the following languages: Inuit, Sanskrit, Tapas and Sudoku.

Mary Ann Bighead

Around the world in 80 columns
Dateline: Mexico

Today is the Day of the Dead Clever where primitive Mexicans celebrate the power of incredibly bright people in an elaborate festival of pagan symbolism and religious ritual.

In the small village where the Bighead family are staying, the locals appear to be worshipping the enormous garishly painted head of an immensely intelligent female, one with beautiful long hair and two very clever children.

When I ask in my fluent Xoxocatalan dialect (very like 11th century Persian as it happens) "Who is this extraordinary woman?" to my embarrassment they all fall to their knees crying, "It is you, Senora Bighead, with your infantos Brainella y Intelligencia!!"

When we return from the Mayan temple to our hotel rooms to have a family evening reading Proust (backwards!) we all agree on what we have learnt. That it is humbling to find, even in a tiny little backwater in the outer reaches of the Mayan civilisation, that ordinary peasants still have a deep-seated respect for people who are very, very, very, very clever!

© The Times

"Our objective is to get to Mars before Tesco does"

21

THOSE PRINCE CHARLES DIARIES

Sensational Extracts From The Secret Journals That Prince Charles Is Trying To Ban

Ying Tong Tiddle I Po, Tuesday

IT REALLY is appalling this handover thingie, pulling down the old flag – mater would be horrified, I mean we're not so bad really, particularly when you look at these ghastly Chinese Johnnies... Pater was right, you know, they do have slitty eyes and they all babble away in some language of their own. I said to friend Patten, "What a shower!" and he said, "Yes, that's because it's the monsoon season, sir!". Honestly, one does one's best, but does one ever get any gratitude? No, of course not. Perhaps they'll appreciate me when I'm deaded! Nicky nacky noo, Jim?!

© His Royal Highness The Prince of Goons, not to be circulated to anyone except people who will tell me how marvellous I am.

How do you like Number Ten?

With beansprouts and fried rice, please

CAMERON RELATED TO EVERYONE

by Our Geneological Staff **Hugh Montgomery Massivesnob**

THE NEW Tory leader, David Cameron, is directly related to all famous people in English history, I can reveal. They range from the Venerable Bede to Nell Gwynne to Camilla Parker-Bowles. Research has shown he is even a distant cousin of Lord Nelson *(81 times removed. Ed)*.

His wife Lady Rowena Starborgling-Cameron is a descendant of Grand Duchess Anastasia of Saxe-Carlsberg via her illegitimate son, Lord Archer of Weston-super-Mare (see the latter's autobiography 'The Story of My Lie', Wormwood and Scrubs, £19.99).

Another distant relative turns out to be Lord Byron, through the marriage of Cameron's great-uncle Sir Charles Moore who famously fell in the Battle of Canary Wharfe, slain by the Black Knight in 2003.

But, most surprising of all, the future Prime Minister of Great Britain is related to the popular entertainers Ant and Dec (real names Sir Anthony Antrobus and Sir Decwell Lozenge who were both contemporaries of Cameron at St Cake's Prep School).

Full story page 94

New Betjeman Poem

The Eye today publishes for the first time the late Poet Laureate's most recent poem, dictated from beyond the grave to his daughter Miss Candida Hunter-Green-Wellington.

> Mrs Camilla Parker-Bowles,
> Mrs Camilla Parker-Bowles,
> Don't you look jolly lovely
> In the back of the Royal Rolls?

(It's not very good, is it, but you can put it in if you like J.B.)

Hear the whole poem, read by Sir Ian McKellen, on www.eyepodcast.com

Cripes, readers! Mr Brillo says I'm not going to edit The Beano any more!!!!

Well he's wrong there!

'Cos I NEVER did! Snigger! Snigger!

COMMONS

TELLY

LEGOVER

DAVE SNOOTY

AND HIS PALS

How dare that oik Davis call me a toff!!

I'm going to give him a damn good thrashing!

On second thoughts, I'll get my fag Gove to do it for me!

BIFF!

POW

WHAT YOU MISSED

That Paxman Cameron Interview in full

Paxman: Oh, come off it!

Cameron: I haven't said anything yet.

Paxman: OK, here's your starter for 10. What's a Pink Pussy?

Cameron: Er...

Paxman: No conferring... Come on! Come on!

Cameron: The new modern Tory Party must...

Paxman: Wrong! You lose five points. The correct answer is, "I'm pathetic, Jeremy, and I should resign at once."

Sound Effect: Bong!

Paxman: So the final score is Cameron (Oxford) 0; Paxman (Cambridge) 167. So congratulations to myself, and we say goodbye to Cameron.

Cameron: Goodbye!

(Ends. Silly music. Credits)

FOOTBALLER DIES

A FOOTBALLER, who became well-known for playing football 40 years ago, has died. *Reuters*

TRIBUTES FLOOD IN FOR GEORGE BEST

by Lifetime O'Booze

FOLLOWING the death of George Best, tributes flooded in from his fellow professional drinkers up and down the country.

"To have seen George Best drinking in his prime was a magical sight," said Old Pete, a tramp fighting with a lamp-post in Manchester. "He could swerve past three or four regulars, leaving them totally bamboozled, to get to the bar first."

"Whether it was scotch, whiskey or vodka, his handling skills were amazing, both at home and of course in Europe where they favour wider-rimmed glasses," said another drinking pal, sleeping on a bench in Liverpool.

"He was so good they had to take one liver off and try another, but he quickly defeated that too."

"Apparently, he was also a footballer, but he never let that get in the way of his drinking," said another drunken pal in Sheffield, urinating into his trousers in tribute."

There will be a minute's silence at all branches of Oddbins on Monday, to mark George's passing.

HYPERBOLICS ANONYMOUS

GEORGE BEST DIES
Ulster Shock

Why's he having a big funeral? He didn't kill anyone

Lives Of The Saints

St George And The Flagon

ST GEORGE is England's best-loved saint, although he was originally born in Northern Ireland. In those times, George was a humble sportsmith who roamed the country kicking a ball around, to the great pleasure of the simple folk of Old Trafford.

Then one fatal day he encountered a large flagon.

"You will never defeat me," quoth the flagon.

"You're right there," said the brave Saint George, "but I'll die trying." He then swallowed the flagon in a single draught. But no sooner had he done so than another flagon appeared, even larger than the first.

"Are you looking at me?" said the flagon. But George showed no fear as he despatched the second flagon. But alas, alack, yet another appeared. And another. And another. And another.

The poor saint fell to his knees, humbly bewailing his fate. "Oh mighty flagon, I can beat various blonden damsels, but verily I cannot beat you".

And so it was that the great knight met his end and George was soon sanctified by his faithful followers and was taken up into the Sky Sports Round-Up.

Lines Written On The Projected Return To The Conservative Party Of The Disgraced Peer, Lord Archer of Weston-super-Mare

BY THE LATE SIR WILLIAM REES-MCGONAGALL

'Twas in the year two thousand and five
That Lord Archer's hopes of a political comeback began to revive,
So he reapplied to join the Tory Party,
Thinking his welcome would be hale and hearty.

After all, had he not served his time,
As penance for his former heinous crime?
Now, surely, he was rehabilitated,
And by his old friends should once again be fêted?

Not so long ago he was London's most glittering host,
Serving his guests Krug champagne and shepherd's pie on toast.
Lady Thatcher, John Major and Sir David Frost,
He entertained them all, regardless of cost.

So still he nurtured his lifelong dream,
That one day he would exercise power supreme.
First he would return in triumph to the House of Peers
When his speeches would be greeted with unanimous 'hear, hears'.

All his past peccadilloes would be forgotten,
And no one would any longer consider him thoroughly rotten.
Nor would they think it was in any way sinister
That he should still aspire to be prime minister.

But, alas, for the dreams of poor old Jeff,
To all his pleadings, the Tories proved deaf.
As he tried to rejoin them, he fell at the very first hurdle,
As the thought of the great novelist made everyone's blood curdle.

And when he listened for the news on Radio Four,
He heard young David Cameron say, "We don't want him any more.
We don't want his sort in the Tories,
He should just go home and write some more of those appalling stories."

So Jeffrey went home and started his new tale,
About a brilliant writer who had been unjustly sent to gaol,
But when he emerged from his incarceration
He proved everyone wrong, and went on to lead a grateful nation.
(That's enough rubbish. Ed.)

© W. Rees-McGonagall.

MONGOL SHOCK

I'm slightly to the right of Genghis Khan

"I hope we're chosen"

SADDAM COURT SHOCK

by Our Man in Iraq **AA Guilty**

NEWS has emerged from Baghdad that Saddam Hussein's victims have once again failed to appear in court.

A legal expert said, "Rumours as to why they haven't bothered attending are rife. Some say they are not happy with the facilities, others say they haven't been allowed enough cigarette breaks – although some believe it might have something to do with the fact that they were butchered to death."

WORD WATCHING

Philip Howard

CELLOTAPH (noun): a large pile of flowers wrapped in cellophane, often with handwritten tributes attached, to mark the death of a public figure whom one has not met (e.g. from BBC News 24, 2005, *"I am standing here in Belfast next to the cellotaph which stretches from here to Stormont"*).

BLEARS (verb): portmanteau word, combining 'bleary', 'blur', 'Blair' and 'liar', to describe method used by ministers to confuse the public (e.g. *"That awful woman blears on and on and on"* ITN News Extra 2005).

COMPASSIONATE (adjective): used to describe young ambitious politicians who stop at nothing to achieve their ends (e.g. *"David is ruthlessly compassionate."* Sky Round-up, 2005).

BLAIR'S CONTROVERSIAL NEW POWER PLAN

by Our Energy Staff **Sally Field** and **Don Jeunesse**

THE Prime Minister last night unveiled his new proposals for power which would, he said, "take Britain into the 22nd Century".

He made clear that there was only one solution to the current shortfall in power and it was not the fashionable option that so-called experts were proposing.

Hot Blair

"Wind isn't the answer," he said, "even though there is a plentiful supply of it close to hand.

"No," he concluded, "the time has come to recommission myself so that I can stay in power well into the future."

His announcement was greeted by a furious protest as one person gathered to voice his concerns.

Said the demonstrator, a Mr Gordon Brown, "Blair power is extremely dangerous and creates huge problems for hundreds of years. It damages the environment and generates vast amounts of toxic waste. Its time is over."

Brown Is New Green

Police were quick to break up the protest on the grounds of Prevention of Terror. Said the Chief Inspector, "Brown could blow up at any moment. He is an accident waiting to happen."

LABOUR CONFERENCE SPECIAL

Speech bubble: I'm having a bad heir day

New Old Sayings

"There's nowt so straight as Robbie Williams"

Traditional Yorkshire Folk Wisdom first recorded 2005

Those Censored Primary School Pictures In Full

Brunel – offending cigar removed

Sir Noel Coward – cigarette holder banned

Exclusive to Private Eye

POETRY CORNER

Lines Written To Commemorate The Award Of The Nobel Prize For Literature 2005 To Myself by *Harold Pinter O.M.*

So. They have given me
The Nobel Prize
For Literature.

That'll show that
Fucking bastard Bush
And his warmongering
Friend Blair.

Wankers.

© *H. Pinter, Winner of the Nobel Peace Prize 2006*

Prize For World's Greatest Living Playwright

BY OUR LITERARY EDITOR ROBERT McCRUMMY

With his latest honour, Harold Pinter joins the pantheon of the greatest writers the world has ever known.

His name now stands alongside such giants of literature as Arne Jokullsson, the Icelandic poet whose epic 20-volume saga, *The Voyage of Moomot*, won him the ultimate accolade in 1943; Sanjit Hatterjee, who won the prize in 1921 for his celebrated Bombay trilogy *Rajput And the Elephant*; and Luigi Umbrello, the Italian Post-Surrealist playwright, winner in 1959 for his still-unperformed play *Six Swedish Bores In Search Of An Author To Give A Prize To.*

Sherlock Holmes – no to pipe

Sir Walter Raleigh, discoverer of tobacco – never existed

What You Will Switch Off This Christmas!

Radio Three presents its 3 month 'Bach-a-thon', the entire works of Johann Sebastian Barking *(is this right? J. Abramsky-Korsakov)*

Christmas Holiday Tuesday

9am *The Christmas Eve Oratorio*, performed by the Orchestra of the European Enlargement, conducted by Jose Manel Barroso.

10.30 *Cantata No.94, Mein Gott Vorsprung Durch Technik*, sung by the Ambrosia Cream Rice Singers accompanied by the Orchestre Glockenspiel of Cracow.

11.00 *Sonata in A*, for Unaccompanied Treble Recorder, BMW 303, soloist: Yoku Tsanami.

12.00 News and weather from Leipzig.

12.05 *St Matthew Parris*, live from Dusseldorf. Orchestra of the Age of Consent with the State Homophobic Chorus.

3.00 Organ Recital from the Cathedral of St Brillo, Padstow. Choral Prelude: *Ich bin ein Classiches FM Lisztner*; Toccata and Fugger: arr. M. Fayed *(cont'd 94 kHz)*.

"Sir, the Surrealist Artist Rifles are going over the top"

Russell.

Simon Hoggart's Hilarious Collection Of Seasonal Round-Robins From Britain's Families!

Dear All,
Well, it's been quite a year for the Quinn Family! Kimberly's gone back to work after a bit of a break to get over all that business with the former Home Secretary and that bastard columnist from the Guardian *(cont. p. 94)*

Dear Friends
What a year for the Blunkett family! David has got a new job working for the Sun (or rather his son, given all the legal bills to pay!), still it's not very hard work this journalism – no wonder that bastard columnist from the Guardian had time to go round shagging Kimberly in the *(cont. p. 94)*

Dear All,
Quite an eventful year for the family Hoggart! Full of amusing, laughable and ridiculous happenings! Things got off to a hilarious start when Simon was revealed to have been *(cont. p. 94)*

POLLY SLAGG

THE GLENDA OF THE GRAUNIAD!!!

■ **ASLAN** – donchahatehim? With his stupid mane and his silly roar and his holier-than-thou goody-two-shoes act!!???? Doesn't he make you want to puke as he goes round sucking up to middle-class children and prosecuting strong, independent women like the white witch??!?

■ GUESS who I've had enough of!?!! Here's a clue!! He's got four legs, a bushy tail and he's trying to brainwash our kiddies!!??? Yes, it's you, Aslan!!! Tell you what, here's a not very hidden message from Auntie Polly – sod off back into the wardrobe where you belong and don't come out again!!??? Geddit??

■ *C.S. LEWIS??!? Donchajust hate him???!*

■ **WARDROBES** – arenchasickofthem??!

■ Lions – Bastards!!! *(Get on with it. Ed.)*

Here they are, Polly's Christmas Creeps!!!

● **Aslan** – he's the stoopid lion from Narnia??!

● **C.S. Lewis** – what a bastard! No wonder he's dead!!!?

● **Aslan** – *(You're fired. Ed.)*

NEW FILMS FOR CHRISTMAS

The Liar, The Witch and The Warmonger

Heartwarming family entertainment with a subtle religious message. Enjoy a fairytale world where nothing is quite what it seems, where weapons magically appear and disappear and where mysterious CIA planes arrive in the night and then fly off to far-away lands.

Eye Rating: Torture!!

"Mum, what's a father?"

QUEUE HERE TO SEE FATHER CHRISTMAS

ROBERT THOMPSON

LETTER TO THE EDITOR
Names of the year

From the Rev. Harold Potter.

Sir, As is customary at this time of year, I have compiled a list of the most popular names given to boys and girls, as recorded in your births column:

	Boys	Girls
1.	Sudoku	Sudoku
2.	Asbo	Narnia
3.	Cameron	Condoleezza
4.	Ayad Allawi	Yasmin Alibhai
5.	Flintoff	Ofili
6.	Ryanair	Katrina
7.	Ottakar	Botox
8.	Voldermort	Vettriana
9.	Aslan	Ulay
10.	Avian	Flu

THE REV. HARRY POTTER,
The Vicarage, St. Hogwarts, Beds.

POETRY CORNER

Lines On The 20th Anniversary Of The Birth Of Mr Wayne Rooney

So. Wayne
Rooney.
You are
20.

"Fuck off!"

That is your
Catchphrase.

> E.J. Thribb (17½ shirt)

In Memoriam Tony Meehan – former member of the Shadows, a popular non-singing group

So. Farewell then
Tony Meehan.

You were one of the
Shadows,
Famous for backing
Sir Clifford
Richard
In such hits as
Living Doll.

Then you left
The group.

Now you are no
Longer living
Yourself.

But you have
Rejoined the
Shadows.

> E.J. Thribb (17½ rpm)

In Memoriam Alida Valli, Italian Film Star Who Played Harry Lime's Girlfriend in *TheThird Man*.

So. Farewell
Then
Alida Valli.

Yes, you
Played Harry Lime's
Girlfriend in *The
Third Man.*

All together
Now –

"Dunka dunka dunk
Ka-Dunk.

Dunka dunka dunk
Ka-Dunk."

Etc.

> E.J. The Thribb Man (78 rpm)

UPFRONTERS

EXCLUSIVE PICTURES FROM
ELTON JOHN'S WEDDING
The stars turn out for the ultimate celebrity do – only in Private Eye!!

The bride is traditionally late but **Liz** made sure she got to the wedding **Hurley**!! She came without you-know-**Hugh**, I'll **Grant** you, but she was every inch the queen of the event – apart from Elton, of course!

It's certainly a **Posh** do! But who has this **Spicy Lady** got at her **Beckham** call! Why, it's none other than **Ronan** who is **Keating** out of her hand! It's a Boyzone adventure but there's no doubt that Victoria is queen of the event – apart from Elton, of course! (*You've done this. Ed.*)

Caine you believe it? **Michael** certainly can't as he goes **Lulu** over this Scottish songbird! Or should we say he goes **Zulu**?! Anyway she certainly looks the queen of the evening – apart from Elton, of course! (*I said you've done this. Ed.*)

Cilla's wearing **Black** to a wedding! Or is it **Donatello Versace**? And who has she linked up with who seems to be right up her **Street-Porter**, why it's **Janet** of course. Unless it's **Paul O'Grady** in drag! Talk about gilding the **Lily Savage**?! Anyway, everyone was agreed that these two were the queens of the evening – apart from Elton, of course! (*Last chance. Ed.*)

These **Boys** don't run a **Pet Shop** you know! Elton's talented musical friends made a lovely couple. Unless they were ex-Beatle **Ringo Starr** and TV chef **Gordon Ramsay**. Or possibly **Paul O'Grady** and **Ronan Keating**? Or lovely **Cilla Black** and sparky **Lulu**? (*I warned you. Ed.*) Either way these two were very much the queens of the evening – apart from Elton and David, of course! (*You're fired. Ed*)

That David Blunkett Today Guest Editorship In Full

Blunkett: So, John Humphrys, do you not agree that in your position you are constantly undermining the democratic process by treating the country's elected representatives with a lack of appropriate respect?

Humphrys: What's your point, Beardie?

Blunkett: The question I'm asking, John, and that you are trying to avoid, is are you or are you not willing to have my babies?

Naughtie: And now Thought for the Day with Sophie.

Dog: Woof!

Blunkett: Thank you very much. Something to think about for us all there. And now with the time coming up to 8.13 we're going over to Annabel's nightclub for an in-depth investigation of the available totty still hanging around (*cont. 94khz*).

SOAP UPDATE
What You Will See

Neighbours BBC1

(*Australian suburb*)

Bruce: Blimey, Sheila, have you seen who's moved in next door?

Sheila: Strewth Bruce! They look like Abos but I think they're Lebs!

Bruce: Shall we invite them round for a barbie!

Sheila: Yeah! And then throw them on it! Bloody towel-heads!

Theme tune: "*Neighbours, Everybody Hates Their Neighbours, Especially if they come from the Middle East*"

ON OTHER PAGES

Why Britain is to blame for this and everything else **by Germaine Greer 94**

"*It had to be put down!*"

POLICE LOG

Neasden Central Police Station
Office hours: 9-12 Mon-Tues (except Tuesday)

7.30am Report to canteen for breakfast. The following items were consumed: 1 so-called 'Neasden Sizzler' consisting of: egg, bacon, sausage, fried bread, beans, black pudding.

The bacon and sausage were optional items with regard to officers of Jewish, Muslim or similar faith orientation, and the black pudding was renamed 'Non-White Pudding' to avoid giving offence to any officers of Afro-Caribbean origin (none).

9.00am Report received that a Mrs Jenny Cardigan had committed a very serious homophobic offence on 'Good Morning Neasden', a local radio station, when she stated in the course of a phone-in interview that in her view many gay men liked Shirley Bassey.

An armed response unit was immediately despatched to Mrs Cardigan's residence at 453 George Melly House, where she was interrogated for seven hours and then cautioned as to her future behaviour.

12.15pm Report received from a Community Support Officer, Ms Dawn Rayde, that while on patrol in the Kofi Annan Shopping Precinct she had observed a gang of uniformed religious extremists playing tubas and singing songs of a highly provocative and offensive nature, such as 'While Shepherds Watched', 'O, Come All Ye Faithful', and 'Silent Night'. The firearms squad was immediately despatched to secure the high street, evacuate the town street and take the terrorist-suspects into custody. The tubas were disposed of by means of a controlled explosion.

5.30pm All officers not otherwise engaged were directed to proceed by vehicular transport in convoy (ie: cars) to Highgrove House, near Tetbury, to interrogate the chief suspect in the murder enquiry relating to Diana, the late Princess of Wales. While proceeding to the interrogation venue via the fast lane of the M94 motorway, a number of other motorists were regrettably killed, owing to the fact that we were travelling at 110 m.p.h., and the aforementioned drivers were impeding our investigation.

On arrival at the home of the suspect, we were informed by a Mr Alan Fitztightly that His Royal Highness was unfortunately not free to be interviewed, since he was in Scotland opening a halal butcher's shop in Auchtermuchty. On returning to the station, officers opened one Christmas hamper generously provided by a Mr A.L. Fayed of the Harrod's Food Department, containing the following: One smoked red herring, One packet Egyptian Delight, One vintage cheese (Gorgon-fuggin-zola), 12 bottles McFayed's Very Old Three-week Matured Whisky ('a wee dram afore ye drive').

8.45pm Report received of an incident involving serious assault, rape and homicide in the George Best Arms public house (formerly the Rose and Crown) opposite the police station. Female caller was advised by automatic answering machine that no officers were available to attend her, owing to prioritising police time in attending other incidents in the locality (see above). She was further advised that counselling services would be made available to her on pressing the hash button on her keypad.

An unforgettable souvenir of the wedding which made history!!

His and His Oven Gloves

THE HOUSE of Gnome is proud to offer a unique memento of the most glorious and important wedding of the 21st century. When Elton and David tied the knot at Windsor Register Office it was a spectacle which will live in our memories for ever. Those who were not fortunate enough to be there in person now have this unique opportunity to share in the joy of that turning point in the history of our island, by purchasing this matching pair of very lovely and wonderful oven gloves

Hand sewn by 5-year-old Chinese craftsmen, from heat-resistant Thermognome (a high-tech material especially developed to allow the EU's Galileo space project to withstand solar wind), these priceless mementos come in a choice of three colours: pink, lilac and pink.

Each glove bears the individualised portrait of one of the civil partners who are now joined together in the same very beautiful way as these heart-warming, heat-resistant oven gloves.

> WARNING: Do not use these commemorative gloves in a hot oven situation

£999.99 for each glove (plus VAT)

Send card details now to:
Gnome Glove Offer, Unit 94, Ojukwu Trading Estate, Lagos, Nigeria
(allow 28 months for delivery).

The Daily Bible

David Floors Goliath with 'Consensus' Tactic

by Our Political Correspondent **Andrew Myrrh**

THE Philistines were reeling last night as new kid on the block David took on their champion and defeated him by agreeing with everything he said.

Goliar

The Philistines were furious at this change in strategy by their opponents' young champion. Said one: "We were expecting him to attack Goliath head-on like all the others have done. It is unfair of him to stand there talking about an end to sling-and-rock politics."

Pundits were, however, unanimous that this was a death blow for the former giant,

Tony Goliar.

"He's finished. David is the future and he's the one who will lead us to the Promised Land."

THE new shadow spokesman on Higher Education writes on the challenges facing the Tertiary Sector in the light of the forthcoming White Paper.

CRIPES! Double Cripes! and Cripes with knobs on! Good old Spliffy Cameron gave me a job after all! Which between you and me rather saved yours truly's bacon because Mr Brillo gave me the old heave-ho as editor of the Beano! Ooh-er!!

So now I've got to bone up on all this brainbox stuff! Higher Education eh? Blimey! That's a tough one, trying to get your noodle round all that! OK, here's my policy. Shooting straight from the hip – why doesn't everyone go to Eton and then on to jolly old Oxford for a spot of getting hog-whimpering drunk down at the Bullingdon Club!!

If it worked for me and Spliffy – why not for everyone else?! Capital idea says I! Cripes! Downing Street here I come!

Chortle, chortle!

© Boris The Menace 2005

DAILY EXPRESS

DIANA'S DEATH
The Proof At Last

Those Daves Write

DAVE SPART (Co-chair of the Tufnell Park Wave Power and Pedestrian Rights Collective)

Er... global warming... sickening third world poverty... er... totally unfettered capitalism... to my mind... er... thatcherist legacy discredited... er... global warming... *(cont. p. 94)*

DAVE CAMERON (Co-chair of the Bullingdon Club and Beagling For All Soc. [Oxon])

Er... global warming... sickening third world poverty... er... totally unfettered capitalism... to my mind... er... thatcherist legacy discredited... er... global warming don'tcha know *(cont. p. 94)*

LIB DEMS NEW YEAR RESOLUTION

We're giving you up

"Ignore it... obviously a mirage"

MOST GRADUATES ILITERATE AND INNUMERABLE

by Our Trainee Staff **Ivor Degree** (B.A. Cantadd)

A SHOCK new report claims that recent graduates are leaving universities "unfit for employment".

Despite achieving good degreez, the graduates are apparently unable to, you know, construct an argument or whatever, which is rubbish, and like, don't understand numbers which is a billion percent wrong at least.

The report claimed that graduates were "indisciplined and unfocused on their work", whatever that means, and is this enough words yet it's time for Countdown on the telly *(You're fired. Ed.)*

GALLOWAY – What On Earth Is He Doing In There?

by Our Political Staff PETER O'BORE

DISILLUSIONED supporters of the television personality George Galloway were last night asking what exactly he thought he was doing by entering the House of Commons.

Said one, "George is a very clever and able man, whatever people say, and to see him degrading himself with this bunch of pathetic self-publicists, deadbeats and misfits is tragic, to my mind.

Celeb Dems

"The sight of George trying to talk about serious issues, such as Iraq or Israel, to some nonentity like Hazel Blears is pathetic."

Said another Galloway fan, "I've got a lot of respect for George. But it is offensive to see him late at night hanging about with a bunch of drunks like Charles Kennedy and former drug addicts such as Dave Cameron.

"Why can't George resist the temptation to preen himself in the House, and knuckle down to his career in television?"

Do you want to see George evicted from the House?

Text us now on 0898-241-241 if you want George to be arrested in connection with the receipt of 2 billion barrels of oil from Saddam Hussein.

Is Nothing Sacred?

asks Britain's leading historian ANDREW ROBERTS

Now I've heard it all. They are going to remake the wartime classic 'They Flew To Bruges'.

I say this. This is sacrilege!

If anything has defined what it means to be British down the centuries then it is this black and white masterpiece which celebrates the men who took part in the most courageous single mission of World War Two – the famous flight to Bruges.

And who could possibly hope to match the unforgettable portrayal of Squadron-Leader Huffington 'Huffy' Buffington by the young John Mills, then at the height of his powers?

Who could equal the young David Tomlinson as Pilot Officer Rollo Rollington?

Or, for that matter, the young Dickie Attenborough as the cheeky daredevil tail-gunner, 'Chalky' Chappie?

They must be stark raving bonkers to think for one minute that they could match the film's now legendary theme tune, the celebrated 'Bruges March', composed by Sir Horace Willmot and later played at the Duke of Gloucester's funeral.

How dare these vandals set out to destroy such an incomparable work of British genius?

Can you imagine the Italians setting fire to the Sistine Chapel, or the French deciding to bulldoze the Eiffel Tower?

Every living patriotic Brit should rise up and say to these Hollywood hooligans – oi, Mr. Film-men, no!

© *Sir Harold Enfield 2005*

On other pages

- Did Bruges Mission Even Take Place? *asks Corelli Barnett,* **10.**
- Should Bruges 'Heroes' Be Tried For War Crimes? *asks Polly Toynbee,* **14.**
- I Always Hated The Film, *says A.N.Wilson,* **36.**

COUNCIL TO BAN VALENTINE'S DAY

by Our Local Government Staff **PC Looney**

THE Midlands council of Market Barkworth has ruled that the town's citizens are not to be permitted to celebrate St Valentine's Day on February 14.

Said the council leader Graham Daft-Bugger, 47, "To celebrate this Christian saint, who probably never existed, could possibly offend Muslims.

"Also," he added, "it is perceived as a heterosexual festival, i.e. it deliberately excludes gays, lesbians and those of trans-gender status, such as myself.

"The good citizens of Market Barkworth are forward-looking, inclusive and modern-minded – they have no time for this kind of sexist elitism based on bigoted and outdated prejudice."

There were angry protests, however, from the Market Barkworth Association of Muslim Newsagents.

Mr Kevin Iqbal, 41, said, "This is political correctness gone mad. The council is trying to destroy our business. Valentine's Day is one of the biggest highlights of the retail calendar, when we expect a high-volume turnover on such items as greeting cards, novelty chocolates shaped as hearts, flowers wrapped in cellophane and special St Valentine Sudoku books for loving couples to do together in bed.

"It is madness gone mad," he continued. "We are lodging an appeal with the European Court of Human Rights. Last year they banned Christmas and Easter. Where will it all end?"

Full story: pp 14-24.

CHILD ISN'T ABDUCTED SHOCK

by Our Social Affairs Staff **Dee Pressing and Sue I. Sidle**

SHOCKING news emerged last night when it was confirmed that a child hadn't been abducted within the last 24 hours.

A police spokesman said, "This is a truly shocking development – I can't remember the last time something as disturbing as this didn't happen."

There were also unconfirmed reports that in the same period a teenager was not raped or murdered, a young man was not fatally stabbed and that apparently an old-age pensioner was not battered to death by relatives. (*Reuters*)

ANTS, A LIFE CYCLE

GRAEME KEYES

WORKER ANT   CONSULTANT   REDUNDANT

THAT RADIO ONE DAVID CAMERON INTERVIEW IN FULL

Russell.

DJ: Hullo and welcome to the studio the leader of the Conservative Party, the Right Honourable David Cameron MP.

Cameron: Cool! Wicked! Minging!

DJ: Mr Cameron can we talk about your education policies – is it true that you favour streaming and setting rather than selection?

Cameron: Scissor sisters!

Coldplay! Kaiser Chiefs!

DJ: Yes but what about grammar schools – surely this is a betrayal of traditional Tory values?

Cameron: Girls Aloud. The Blonde One. Cor! Eh?

DJ: I gather you have also confirmed your support for the NHS in its current form?

Cameron: Little Britain! Catherine Tate! Ricky Gervais!

DJ: On a lighter note, I suppose I have to ask you about pop.

Cameron: Yes absolutely I was a member at Eton along with Boris Johnson and Ollie Nitwit and Charlie Moore. Bloody good fun! You could wear these spliffing waistcoats with your top hat and tails doncha know?

(The interview had to be terminated at this point when a number of advisors put a sack over Mr Cameron's head and bundled him into a waiting van).

Notes & Queries

QUESTION: Why is the acting Liberal leader Sir Menzies Campbell known as "Ming"?

□ IT IS a little-known fact that Sir Menzies, although brought up in Scotland, was born in China, where he came from a long line of Oriental newsagents.

Sir Menzies has never denied that he is Chinese, and those who know him well invariably call him "Ming The Useless", after the 15th century leader who briefly occupied the Imperial "Rib Dem" throne, after the assassination of Cha Lee, known as "The Inebriated".

"No. Look at the queues... we'd be ages"

INSTANT GRATIFICATION!! GET IT HERE!! RIGHT NOW!!

EXCLUSIVE TO THE DAILY MAIL

What do they have to hide?

LABOUR was last week accused of running scared from a potentially devastating public inquiry into the July 7 attacks in London.

But why are they refusing to hold such an inquiry?

Many vital questions remain unsolved. The most pressing include:

Why weren't any members of the cabinet killed in the attack? Was it because they were "warned" they would take place?

Were the bombers coached and trained to carry out these deadly attacks in Number 10 by Cherie Blair?

Was John Prescott the fifth bomber?

Of course the answer to all these questions is "no", but we wish with every fibre of our being that it was yes *(cont. col 94, p94.)*

Coming soon – the film they tried to ban!

A CHOCOLATE ORANGE

based on Michael Gove's best-seller "Towards a New Conservatism"

A terrifying picture of Britain in the near-future, where a gang of disaffected youths go round branches of W.H. Smith telling the managers to replace chocolate oranges with fresh fruit – or face the consequences!

Meet "Dave", the ultra-smooth gang leader, whose outward charm conceals a ruthless desire for power.

Around him we see the most frightening gang Britain has ever known, "Gove", "Olly", "Gumbag", "Zac", "Two Brains" and, most terrifying of all, "Boris", the blond sex-fiend who will stop at nothing to get attention!

"It certainly scares the pants off me!"
Simon Heffer, *Daily Telegraph*

WHY KENNEDY HAD TO GO

by Lunchtime O'Booze, Dinnertime O'Booze and Breakfast Time O'Booze

YES it's sad – but it was inevitable. Charles Kennedy could no longer hide from the truth. When a man drinks so much that he cannot do his job, it is time to admit it and retire gracefully.

The spectacle of a middle-aged drunk slurring hish wordsh and repeating himshelf and slurring hish wordsh and repeating himshelf is a pitiful shite and cannot be tolerated except in journ…journ…jono…

except in the presh.

Sweating, shaking and looking like death, I asked Charles Kennedy if my career was over.

Same Piece Again Please

It says everything about the state of politics today that I have no idea what his reply was.

Still. In the end I knew it was time to go. To the toilet. And then maybe back to the bar for just one more. Line 'em up barman! You're my best friend. Yesh you are. D'you know my editor doesn't understand me? © All newspapers.

"When can you start?"

Daily Mail

FRIDAY, JANUARY 20, 2006

WHY WAS THIS WOMAN ALLOWED TO WORK WITH CHILDREN?

by Our Education Staff **A Star**

A HUGE row yesterday engulfed Education Secretary Ruth Kelly, 25, when it was revealed that she had been given a top job running a ministry despite the fact that everyone involved knew she was useless.

There are extensive checks and guidelines to ensure that unsuitable characters are kept away from posts connected with children's education.

But in this case it seems all these safety measures were deliberately ignored.

Yet the man responsible for this disastrous system failure, Mr Tony Blair, 53, claims that it was not his decision and that he "knew nothing about it".

The Mail asks: How many other useless politicians have been appointed to top jobs in education?

Is it not time to reopen the files on such previous appointments in this highly sensitive area as David Blunkett, Charles Clarke or even the self-styled "Lord Adonis"?

LIB DEMS SALUTE BRAVE CHARLES

You've got a lot of bottle

You'll be sorely pissed

You were the George Best leader the party has ever had

The BBC Presents

ROME

An extraordinary tale of power, lust and depravity, set at the turn of the 21st Century.

(Tousle-haired Roman patrician in Old Etonian toga sits at his desk, working on his important speech to the Senate)

Boris Absurdicus *(for it is he)*:
Blimeus! Cripus! This jolly old Roman Empire works pretty damn well, eh? Much better than the EU, whatever that is

going to be!! And Cameronius – what a spliffing chap he is! We were at collegium together! Floreat myself what!

(Enter gorgeous, pouting, aristocratic Roman lovely)

Boris: Ave Petronella! You must be a vestal virgin.

Petronella: And you must be joking!

(Ends)

Cast In Full

BORIS ABSURDICUS..........Frankie Howerd

PETRONELLA WYATTUS....Barbara Windsor

CAMERONIUS MAXIMUS..............Jim Dale

RODUS LIDDLUS.............Charles Hawtree

ST CAKES IN 'PAEDOPHILE TEACHER' ROW

by Our Education Staff **Noncy Bonks-Smith**

THE headmaster of St Cakes, the prestigious £30,000-a-term independent boarding school for boys (motto 'Ave Matelotus!'), has admitted that he employed a teacher who is not on the sex offenders' register.

Said a clearly embarrassed Mr R.G.J. Kipling, "It has been brought to my attention that the teacher in question, Mr Straight-Trouser, is under no suspicion at all of being a paedophile. I can only apologise to parents," he continued, "for this appalling oversight. It will not happen again."

Mr Straight-Trouser has been suspended as Master of Buggers and replaced as music teacher by Mr G. Glitter who comes to the school highly recommended by the Thai police authority.

33

The Alternative Rocky Horror Service Book

No. 94 A Service for Easter Day

President: Brothers and sisters, we are gathered together here today or, rather, most of us are, except the Bishop obviously, who is very busy on his cruise around the Mediterranean.

All: Bastard!

President: Thanks be to Swan Hellenic.

All: Not!

Hymn

(There shall then be sung a traditional hymn, "For Those We Hope Are In Peril On The Sea")

Reading

(There shall then follow a reading from the Old Testament)

"And Jonah was enjoying his freebie cruise, stopping off at Joppa and Tarshish and spent his time eating at the Captain's table, giving the odd lecture and catching the International Cabaret featuring the Sodom and Gomorrah Dancers. However, a great storm arose making Jonah and his wife feel really sea-sick for days because God was clearly pretty angry that Jonah wasn't getting on with his job as Bishop of Nineveh. And then guess what? He sent a huge whale to swallow Jonah up, which served him jolly well right."

President: This is the word of the Lord.

All: Are you listening, Beardy?

The Sermon

(There shall follow a short address, not by the Bishop, obviously, on the theme "Omnipresence: Why only God can be in two places at once")

The Dismissal

President: The Bishop should be dismissed.

All: Dismissing is too good for him.

(The congregation shall then process out to the accompaniment of Sir Clifford Richard's anthem "We're Not Going On An Easter Holiday")

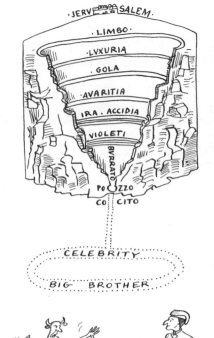

"Sorry, Signor Dante, we've had to add another circle..."

The 10 Things Which Best Define What It Is To Be English

After years of consultation and research, the Department for Culture, Media and Sport has produced a definitive list of national icons, to help everyone feel that they belong in a very real sense to the England of the 21st century.

Those 10 Tell-tale Icons in Full

1. Big Ben. Historic symbol of English democracy. Always right.

2. Tony Benn. Historic symbol of English democracy. Always left.

3. Chicken Tikka Massala. Historic symbol of English cuisine down the ages.

4. Thierry Henry. Timeless symbol of English football at its best.

5. Sudoku. Timeless symbol of Englishman's love of puzzles.

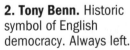

6. Budweiser lager. Historic symbol of the Englishman's love of getting drunk and being sick in town centres.

7. The Honda Civic. The fashionable English car whose design epitomised the Swinging Nineties.

8. Jamie Oliver's 'Cooking the Italian Way'. Known as the 'Englishman's Food Bible'.

9. The M25 Motorway. Timeless architectural symbol of the Englishman's love of the countryside.

10. Princess Michael of Kent. The fragrant English rose who is the most loved member of Britain's Royal family.

11. The Ikea Furniture Centre, Brent Cross. The ultimate English retail experience for which tourists come from across the world.

12. *(That's enough icons, Ed.)*

THIEVES GET AWAY WITH RECORD HAUL IN DARING HEIST

by Our Crime Staff **Phil Swag**

CRIMINALS pretending to be British Gas officials made off with a staggering £1.5 billion yesterday in the most audacious raid Britain has ever seen.

The thieves, posing as energy suppliers, held the public to ransom and then grabbed an astonishing one-and-a-half billion pounds in cash – in broad daylight.

"It was so simple," said one astonished victim. "They sent me a bill and threatened to cut me off if I didn't pay it." He continued, "I've got a wife and kids, so I had no option but to give in to their demands."

The mastermind behind the crime is believed to be an "insider" with detailed knowledge of how a supplier of essential services can charge as much as it likes and get away with it.

Last Will And Testament
SIR EDWARD HEATH

I, Sir Edward Aloysius 'Grocer' Heath, being of sound mind, do hereby bequeath the following items as set out below:

To Mrs H. Prunehat, in thanks for 40 years' faithful service as housekeeper, the sum of £9.99.

To Mr P. Barnfather, in thanks for 25 years' faithful service as my chauffeur and handyman, the sum of £5.35.

The remainder of my estate (£5 million) will be devoted to the setting up, in my former very fine and much admired home at 1, The Close, Salisbury, of the 'Sir Edward Heath Memorial Museum and Centre for Edward Heath Studies'. This will contain the following exhibits, to be displayed in perpetuity for the edification of future generations of students from all over the world, viz:

1 conductor's baton, as used by myself when conducting the Peking Democratic People's Orchestra in a performance of "*The Hullo Sailor's Hornpipe*" (arr. Heath) in 1979.

1 photograph in silver frame, showing myself standing next to the Rev. Sun Moon Loon, with 30,000 happy Korean newly-weds in the background.

1 very rare unsigned copy of my best-selling book "*Sailing*".

1 souvenir "Voodoo" doll, showing the late prime minister, Mrs Margaret Thatcher, with a number of coloured pins inserted into particularly painful points of her anatomy – a gift from the late President "Papa Doc" Duvalier of Haiti.

Also to be made available to serious scholars, a unique collection of 3 million documents and letters relating to my finest achievement, ie, the negotiation of the historic European Single Fish Treaty of 1972.

EXCLUSIVE TO EYE READERS

THE GNOME HOME SCOOP KIT

Fooling celebrities is easy, thanks to this simple DIY journalist outfit!

Includes:

- ✓ **Tea towel**
- ✓ **White robe**
- ✓ **Spray-on tan**
- ✓ **False beard**
- ✓ **Bottle of champagne**
- ✓ **Tape-recorder in briefcase**

ALL you have to do is book a hotel room and invite your favourite greedy celebrity to come round and, hey presto, scoop's in the bag!

How it will sound:

Fake Arab *(you)*: Hello, celebrity, would you like a million pounds?

Celebrity: Yes, please. I'm very stupid and greedy.

Fake Arab *(you)*: Can you be rude about everyone you know, please – into this briefcase?

Celebrity: Yes, of course. I'll do anything for money.

Fake Arab *(you)*: Allah be praised!

Send now for fully-guaranteed kit for only £99.99 (plus p&p) to: Gnome Sting Offer, Unit 94, The Mazher Mahmood Trading Estate, Birmingham.

SVEN IN AMAZING HOAX

35

'YES, I'M LIB DEM' Admits Gay MP

by Our Westminster Staff **Lunchtime O'Boys**

IN A sensational disclosure last night, a well-known homosexual member of Parliament was forced to admit to a tabloid newspaper that for years he had been an active Liberal Democrat.

Said the MP, "I have always believed that my political life is my own affair, and that the press has no right to know what I do in public."

After years of denying that he was a Lib Dem, the MP had been confronted by the Sun's political correspondent, Trevor Git, with photographic evidence obtained at a conference in Llandudno, showing him openly consorting with known Lib Dems, such as Mark Oaten and Simon Hughes.

Oaten Beam

He was also secretly tape-recorded using his mobile phone to contact Lib Dem voters, inviting them to "come out" and join him in what the newspaper described as "third-party activities too unpleasant to mention in a respectable newspaper".

LIB DEM IN THREE-IN-A-PARTY SHOCK

by Our Political Staff **Phil Bottom**

A SENIOR MP confessed last night that he had indulged in a threesome with fellow Liberal Democrats.

"Yes, it's true," he said. "There are only three members of the party left since everyone else has resigned in disgrace."

He admitted that the three of them had indulged in "humiliating practices" such as discussing Liberal policy on taxation, and had lived out their "perverse fantasies" of forming a government.

THE DAILY TELEGRAPH

Letters *to the Editor*

SIR – Like many of your readers, I was shocked and appalled by the story of Mr Mark Oaten and the rent-boys. How the standards of public life have fallen! In my day, a rent-boy could be relied upon to maintain a discreet silence regarding the identity and predilections of their clients, particularly where three-in-a-bed romps are concerned. Things have come to a pretty pass when a man cannot even indulge in an afternoon of innocent homosexual dalliance, without the news reaching his wife and children courtesy of the popular press.
Sir Hugo Gaytrouser,
The Athenaeum.

SIR – Like many of your readers, I was shocked and appalled by the government's plan to legalise the running of so-called 'mini brothels'; where a maximum of two 'sex workers' may be permitted to practise their trade without interference. How the standards of public life have fallen! In my day, a brothel was a large and well-appointed establishment, efficiently run by a well-qualified 'madame', offering a wide range of agreeable young ladies who could provide an extensive choice of personal services. To think that the once distinguished term 'brothel' can now be demeaningly applied to some dingy Soho bedroom, where two dismal East European drug-addicts can fuel their habit by offering me 'executive relief' at an exorbitant fee of £90 (including VAT) is little short of scandalous.

No wonder we are the laughing stock of Europe!
Obadiah Rees-Beeswax Q.C.,
Lincoln's Inn.

Long Tradition Of Sodomy In Gladstone's Liberal Party

by **Sir Anthony Howard**

THE CURRENT spate of revelations concerning the sexual proclivities of leading members of the Liberal Party will come as no surprise to those of us whose political memories stretch back further than the most recent episode of Big Brother.

Setting aside for a moment the continuing historical speculation over the private life of the Earl of Rosebery, we have only to think of the example set by the most famous leader of the party in recent times, Sir Jeremy Fisher.

It is now 25 years since the newspaper-reading public were entertained by bizarre revelations concerning Sir Jeremy's relations with a large fish while dressed in a seedy rubber macintosh and galoshes *(Is this right? Wasn't there something about a dog? Ed.)*

Lemsip The Kingmaker Backs Thorpe

by **Alan Watneys**

MR OPEC LEMSIP, 22, the distinguished Lib Dem backbencher and husband of famous TV weather girl Myfanwy Isobar, has revealed that he is now backing 87-year-old Jeremy Thorpe for the leadership of the party.

Previously, Mr Lemsip had pledged "101 percent support" for Mr Charles Glenmorangie, switching subsequently in quick succession to Mr Mark Outed, Mr Simon Oohs and Mr Ming Vase, the Sino-Scottish newsagent. But, following the withdrawal of all the candidates, Mr Lemsip has announced that he is calling for the return of the party's former leader Jeremy Thorpe.

"What the party now needs above all," he said, "is someone who has no skeletons in his closet, and isn't going to be revealed doing something embarrassing, such as attempting to murder a gay lover on Exmoor.

"Jeremy is the man for the job. He is what I call a safe pair of trousers."

Lemsip Opec is 15.

Liberals traditionally have a beard

A Doctor Writes

Should they be allowed to die without any dignity?

IS IT fair that we as a mature sophisticated nation allow the Liberal Democratic Party to kill themselves in a painful, protracted and humiliating way?

Surely we should permit this elderly and weak party to terminate themselves in private with some modicum of *(cont. p94)*

A Yellow Taxi Driver writes

Every week a well-known yellow cabbie is invited to give his views on an issue of topical importance.

THIS WEEK: **Simon Hughes MP**, Cab No. 737428, on Homosexuality.

Blimey, those poofs, eh, guv? What a disgrace! That Peter Tatchell, he should be strung up! It's the only language he understands. You wanna go STRAIGHT there, guv? I'm your man. No cruising around Old Compton Street with me, mate. Where was I? Oh, yes, poofs – well, fair enough, live and let live, none of our business what they get up to, is it? Not that I'd know of course. Blimey, who's that coming up my exhaust pipe? No, thanks, mate! Anyway, where was I? Oh yes, poofs – what's the problem? I drive on both sides of the road, who doesn't? Fancy going to Old Compton Street? Suit yourself, luv. I had that Peter Tatchell in the back of the cab – what a sweetie! Excuse me, I've just gotta do a huge u-turn.

© *A yellow cabbie.*

'THIS COURT DOES NOT EXIST,' Claims Historian

by Our Legal Staff **Joshua Rosenbeard**

Austria, Thursday

MR DAVID IRVING, the well-known historian, provoked a storm of controversy yesterday when he denied the existence of the three-year prison sentence he had just been handed down by an Austrian court.

"There are no gaols in Austria," he told waiting newsmen, "and there never have been. It was all made up by American Jews."

Irving Berliner

However, five minutes later, Mr Irving admitted that he had changed his mind, after examining new evidence. "I now accept," he said, "that this prison may well exist, and that millions of innocent historians are being put to death here for telling the truth."

(Full story p. 94)

"I'm from the lesbian squat next door, can I borrow a cup of semen?"

That New Over-75s Driving Test In Full To Ensure They Are Fit For Today's Roads

When someone cuts you up a roundabout, do you wind down the window and...

a) scream foul-mouthed racial abuse at them?

b) give them the finger, then spit at them?

c) brandish the baseball bat you keep under the seat threatingly at them?

d) All of the above.

You are approaching a pedestrian crossing. A woman pushing a pram has just stepped out onto it. Do you...

a) speed up, start blowing your horn and laugh as she scrambles back onto the pavement?

b) not notice her because you're out of your head on drink and drugs?

c) All of the above.

You are snapped by a speed camera while doing 60 mph in a 30 mph zone. What do you use to smash the speed camera to pieces when you return there in the dead of night?

a) a hammer?

b) a pick-axe?

c) a JCB digger?

d) All of the above.

(That's enough modern driving test. Ed)

TV Highlights

Is The Documentary About The Death Of The Sitcom Dead? *BBC2*

ALAN YENTOB introduces a film which explores the theory that the documentary charting the demise of the sitcom has finally had its day. With dull clips from all the other classic sitcom documentaries and contributions from Alan Yentob, Alan Yentob and Alan Yentob.

NEXT WEEK: The History Of The Spoon. Alan Yentob looks at the role of the spoon in design history and poses naked with only a spoon covering up his (That's enough. Ed.)

I'M SO HAPPY I COULD EXPLODE!

HAMAS WIN THE ELECTION

Those Palestinian Election Results In Full

Gaza, West

Shufti al Kruk (*The Fatah Catah Party*) 2,742; **Khillal Juze** (*Hamasmurder Party*) 47,302; **Mr George Galloway** (*Pro-Saddam Anti-Jodie-Marsh Alliance*) 0. Hamas elected. Galloway voted out.

West Bank (East)

Mustafa Bakhanda (*Fatah Cheque-in-Bank*) 1,302; **Mahmoud al assassin** (*Hamasgrave*) 7,402; **Ali Shirt Liftah** (*Liberal Democrat*) 0. No change as Hamas candidate "taken out" by Mossad. Lib Dem stoned to death.

PALESTINIAN ELECTION SHOCK

Democracy doesn't mean voting for whoever you want

HAMAS OFFER

THE new Hamas Government in Gaza has insisted that it is ready to meet with Israel despite the Israeli announcement of punitive sanctions against it.

"Our representatives are prepared to travel to the West Bank at any time, carrying fresh proposals for peace wrapped around the dynamite strapped to their waists" said a Hamas (cont. p. 94)

Nursery Times

Friday, February 17, 2006

NEVERLAND REJOICES AT HOOK ARREST

by J.M. Barrie-Fantoni

THE Neverland police finally swooped on the most notorious pirate in Neverland, Captain Hook, after keeping him under "close surveillance" for over 100 years.

Said Chief Inspector Wendy Darling, "After studying millions of hours of CCTV footage of the alleged pirate, we at last feel we have enough evidence to charge him."

Rum Do

Hook appears, inciting his followers to engage in acts of piracy, ordering small children to walk the plank, and brandishing a cutlass in a manner likely to cause a breach of the peace.

When asked why the police had failed to act earlier against a man who was clearly a dangerous pirate, Chief Inspector Darling explained, "We have to maintain a very delicate balance between doing something and doing nothing. We chose to do nothing, which is what we call 'smart policing'."

On Other Pages

● Darling Children Taken Into Care **2**

● "My coke-fuelled love romps with Peter Pan" by Tinkerbell **8**

PLUS

● Our page 3 Lagoon Lovelies – mermaids as you've never seen them.

HAMZA PLEADS INNOCENCE

I had no hand in terrorism

EYE PROBE

IS THERE AN ABU HAMZA IN YOUR STREET?

10 Tell-tale signs that your next-door neighbour could be a dangerous terrorist

1 Bushy black beard.

2 Squinty eyes.

3 Funny teeth.

4 Hook instead of hand.

5 10,000 videos of himself inciting huge crowds of followers to commit mass murder.

6 Electric toothbrush easily convertible into rocket launcher.

7 Cartoon in front window showing Jews being eaten by pigs.

8 Rough Guide to the 'Top 100 Places in Europe to Blow Yourself Up' *(published by 72 Virgin Press).*

9 Discount card for local massage parlour ('Hook Jobs a Speciality' – reduced terms for the disabled).

10 1 copy of the Sunday Telegraph crossword half completed.

WARNING
If you have a Hamza-style world terrorist leader living on your doorstep, ring the police at once and within only 10 years they might just possibly come round to arrest him, although it is more likely that they will come round immediately to arrest you for inciting racial hatred.

Play The New Game Sweeping The Balkans

WHERE'S MLADIC?

The former Serb warlord has skilfully blended into the crowd in this typical Belgrade fair. Can you do what the Serbian authorities and U.N. can't... and find him?

THOSE SERBIAN RESPONSES

Thousands of Muslims murdered   **One Milosevic not murdered**

IN THE COURTS
Regina v. Charles
Day 94

Before Mr Justice
Cocklecarrot

Sir Ephraim Hugefee Q.C.
(acting for His Royal Highness the Prince of Wales): My Lord, I shall in this case be seeking to show that the action of the Mail on Sunday, in publishing the article "Barmy Chazza Does His Royal Nut", constituted a prima facie instance of breach of confidence, contract, copyright and consanguintendum magnatum as grave as any such case as has ever been presented to the courts of this land.

Mr Justice Cocklecarrot *(for it is he)*: I shall be the judge of that, Sir Ephraim!

Sir Ephraim: I am indebted to Your Lordship. I would ask the court to look at Bundle B, containing the manuscript of a private diary, written by His Royal Highness and circulated to a few hundred close friends, on the strict condition that the document was to remain confidential until everyone mentioned in the diaries was dead. Indeed, the cover bore the words "For Your Slitty Eyes Only", clearly a jocular reference to the fact that the subject matter of the diary was a vital, top-level diplomatic mission to the People's Republic of China.

Cocklecarrot: To what point are you leading, Sir Ephraim? Can we not immediately proceed to the highly sensitive and diplomatically embarrassing bits?

Sir Ephraim: I refer to the entry for May 4, in which His Royal Highness writes: "I am on my way to Hong Kong, to give it away to what Pater would call 'our yellow friends'. They seem to have put me in something called 'Club Class' (!), where the chairs are very small. And they've no idea how to do an organic cucumber sandwich. One has to eat it from a kind of plastic box thingie, and there's no one there to open it for you. It really is appalling (!)"

Cocklecarrot: Is there much more of this stuff, Sir Ephraim?

Hugefee: 942 pages, to be precise, your honour. I now draw your attention to paragraph 47B on page 212, where His Highness begins with the words "It really is appalling".

Cocklecarrot: Yes, it really is appalling, isn't it?

(Court dissolves in appreciative laughter at this sally of judicial wit)

Hugefee: Indeed, Your Honour. The next thing that His Highness finds appalling is the fact that the Prime Minister seems to have no ideas of his own and has some very second-rate advisers.

"This Blair chap is a perfectly nice fellow. He listened to everything I said, and even nodded once or twice as he closed his eyes to concentrate on what I was telling him about the dangers of GM crops. It really is appalling, I told him."

Cocklecarrot: Do we really have to listen to all this "appalling" stuff again?

(Court is swept by gales of laughter at this further instance of the judge's comedic gift)

Hugefee: M'Lud, I am obliged to spin this out until it is time for luncheon, however thin our case may seem. May I move on to paragraph 78C on page 512?

"We have finally arrived in Hong Kong which, even though it is British, is full of Chinese people (a bit like Soho!). I am here to hand it back to President Chow Mein, or whatever his name is, so that the ghastly Communists can ruin it. Although to be honest, it's almost ruined already, with all its hideous tower blocks ruining the skyline!"

My Lord, I submit that it is not hard to imagine the feelings of my client when he saw these private thoughts blazoned shamelessly across the pages of the gutter press..

Cocklecarrot: All this talk of Chinamen has reminded me, Sir Ephraim, that they are currently offering a special Chinese New Year celebratory luncheon at the Garrick Club, and it would therefore be sensible to adjourn at this point, in order not to miss the dim sum.

Hugefee: I trust you are not referring to my client as a "dim son", or I shall be forced to sue you as well. Ha, ha, ha... *(No one joins in this laughter.)*

Cocklecarrot : I make the jokes around here, Sir Hugefee.

(Court convulses in sycophantic laughter. National anthem plays, as all exit for luncheon.)

Advertisement

GNOME SPECIAL OFFER

TO celebrate the genius of Mozart on the 250th anniversary of his birth *(or death – subs, please check)*, Lord Gnome is proud to offer the readers of Private Eye the **MOZART DUVET COVER**

This very beautiful drip-dry Gnomelene duvet cover, bearing an exact facsimile of the type of notes Mozart would have used in one of his famous pieces of music, is guaranteed to keep "fans" "cosi" for "tutti" the night long!!

● *Designed by the world's leading duvet cover artist, Arvo Toggle (RBDG), your duvet cover will be a treasured heirloom for years to come!!*

Send now to: Gnome Mozart Offer, c/o The World of Duvets, The Trading Estate, Solihull.

The BLACK Mail
ON SUNDAY

THE events in a London courtroom this week have starkly revealed that Prince Charles should keep his opinions to himself.

Why did the Prince foolishly choose to go public with his crackpot views by writing them in a private journal?

Surely he must have realised that his personal staff would have no choice but to steal the journal and sell the contents to us for a tidy sum.

The next time the Prince chooses to go public in this fashion, he should perhaps first reflect on the damage such a rash decision will have upon him.

And a last thought. Why on earth should the unelected Prince seek to have any influence over political matters? Politics should be left to the democratically-elected editors of national newspapers, like myself. *(Shurely shome mishtake? Ed.)*

© *Blackmail on Sunday*

MUSLIMS CALL FOR DAY OF ANGER

by Our Cartoon Staff **Terry Fide**

MILITANT Islamic groups in Britain have called for a day of anger at the outrageous behaviour of the British media who have given them no excuse to be angry.

"It is a disgrace," said spokesman Imamad Bastahdi. "The British newspapers have blatantly refused to print the offensive cartoons and the TV stations only showed them for a couple of seconds.

"How on earth are we meant to get offended, whip up a mob and demand that everyone involved be murdered?"

Mr Bastahdi also said that Muslims like himself were furious at the British Government who had denounced the Danish cartoonists and also at the British police who had quite deliberately failed to arrest anyone for incitement to murder.

"It is a conspiracy by the entire British establishment to deny us our fundamental human rights to go berserk, burn down buildings and threaten to kill people.

*"Sound the alarm – it's the Danes and they've brought **cartoonists** with them!"*

Advertisement

new from mullahcare

The I ♥ Al-Qaida Hat

Your little one will look quite terrifying in this shocking beanie hat. Comes with matching 'Behead The Infidel' babygrow and matching booties, one saying '9' and one '11'!

Exclusive to mullahcare
Your one-stop shop for all baby's pro-terrorist outfits!

LEMMINGS PROTEST AT CARTOON INSULT

by Our Media Staff **Cliff Top**

THE International Lemming Association has threatened mass protests at what it described as "grotesque stereotyping" of the Lemming Community by western cartoonists.

Said a spokesman "It is very offensive to depict lemmings as mindless creatures following their leaders to commit suicide by jumping off a cliff."

"These images of so-called suicide lemmings are an insult to all decent lemmings and are designed to propagate a false impression of lemmings."

He continued "Now if you'll excuse me, I can see one of my colleagues jumping off a cliff and I must go and follow him."

POLICE LOG

Neasden Central Police Station
Office hours: 9-12 Mon-Tues (except Tuesday)

0428 hrs PC Blenkinsop reported in after test-driving a police vehicle the wrong way round the North Circular, between Exit 10 (Ballsover by-pass) and Exit 12 (World Of Fences). He reported having achieved an average speed in excess of 159 mph, thus breaking the station record previously held by the late PC Forsyth (146 mph). Blenkinsop incurred only 3 civilian casualties during his five-minute drive and has been recommended for promotion.

0800 hrs Applications were considered for would-be recruits to the Neasden force. Of the 612 applicants, 552 were disqualified immediately on the grounds that they were white, male, physically fit and in all other ways met the requirements for the job. Following Home Office guidelines, the successful applicants were eventually narrowed to three, all of whom conformed to the new guideline specifications: i.e. they were disabled, of ethnic descent, were members of the transgender community and were educationally challenged. They also showed familiarity with the justice system, as they all had distinguished criminal records. The successful candidates were welcomed to our team in the canteen during our customary mid-morning break (1000-1200 hrs). Mrs Prendergast, our canteen assistant, was placed under arrest for serving Danish bacon, a clear attempt to incite religious hatred against the Muslim members of the force (none). Mrs Prendergast was later admitted to hospital after suffering an unfortunate fall in the cells.

1245 hrs Call received from the proprietor of the Londis store in Heathcoat-Amory Street to the effect that he had detained a shoplifter in possession of 12 jars coffee (Fair Trade, decaff), 6 packets Hobnob biscuits, 1 VHS cassette ('Come On The Squirrels, A History of Neasden FC'), 2 packets Dairylea Cheese-Style Slices, 1 copy Nuts magazine and 1 packet of Werther's Originals. The total value of the items was estimated to be £43.75, placing them well below the new £75 threshold necessary to establish that an offence has been committed. A 12-man armed response unit was immediately despatched to arrest the manager, Mr Ganesh, for wasting police time. His arrest was duly enforced with very few civilian casualties. The alleged "shoplifter" was given a lift back to his hostel and offered counselling following the breach of his human rights. Two para-legal community support officers were detailed to assist him in preparing a compensation claim against Mr Ganesh.

1430 hrs Following representations from the Neasden Jihad League, all available officers were instructed to escort members of the League on their planned demonstrations at the premises of the Danish furniture company Ikea. The purpose of the police escort was to protect the protestors' right to display placards carrying such slogans as "Kill The Infidels", "We Want Holocaust Now!" and "Death To The Cartoonists!" It was necessary to ensure their freedom of protest against any interference by members of the public. During the demonstration a number of arrests were made involving persons who were seeking to incite religious hatred against the protestors by engaging them in dialogue. These included the Rt Rev Moses Sentanugu, the Bishop of Neasden, Rabbi Rachel Coren of the Liberal Reformed Orthodox Synagogue in Pricerite Road, and Dr Sylvester Dawkins, Chair of the Neasden Chapter of the Seventh-Day Atheists. The peaceful demonstration went off without further incident, apart from the setting fire to the premises of Messrs Ikea & Co, the unfortunate Swedish retailer, and the beheading of a small number of the firm's staff.

1930 hrs The station was closed to permit all officers to attend a "gala dinner" at the Star Of Basra restaurant, to celebrate the acquittal of PCs Trigger and Happy on charges of homicide, following their shooting of a member of the public for carrying a dangerous chair leg. A toast was drunk to the two officers in honour of their great victory, and they were granted six months' compassionate golfing leave in the Algarve.

CLASSIC TALES FROM DENMARK
by Hans Muslim Anderson

No. 94 The Little Match Girl

ONCE upon a time there was a little girl who set fire to the Danish Embassy and went to heaven.
(*The End*)

*"Remember the good old days when you were scared of **me**?"*

IRAQ JOINT PLANNING COMMITTEE

STAY IN   PULL OUT

HUNTer

Lookalikes

Einstein   **Lynam**

Sir,
It is good to see that the new presenter of the 'Countdown' TV programme on Channel 4 is Albert Einstein. More than a match for Carol Vorderman I would think.
How fortunate he has a striking resemblance to the presenter Des Lynam. Are they by any chance related?

Yours sincerely,
NOEL TOMLINSON,

Hull, E. Yorks.

Sideshow Bob   **Phil Spector**

Sir,
Perhaps Bart was wrong, and Sideshow Bob really was innocent of robbing the Kwik-E-Mart. There is, after all, more than a passing resemblance. Perhaps we will be told?

KEN TOUGH,

Via email.

Captain   **Angel**

Sir,
Has anyone noticed the likeness between Raphael's Angel and England's Captain, Michael Vaughan?

Yours sincerely,
ANNA WEBSTER,

Toynton All Saints, Lincs.

Prescott   **Everglot**

Sir,
"Two Shags" Prescott and Finnis Everglot – one, father of the Corpse Bride; the other, father of another episode in the Labour landslide into sleaze. But who could have spawned these two? We must be told.

STEPHEN CARR,

Harborne, Birmingham.

Data   **David Cameron**

Sir,
While watching Star Trek: the Next Generation on DVD I was shocked by the chilling similarity of the intergalactic android Data to prospective Tory leader David Cameron. Is there a message in this about the future face of politics?

Yours worryingly,
GIUSEPPE ALBANO,

Via email.

Royle   **Hussein**

Sir,
You never see them in the same place at the same time...

Yours bemusedly,
CORRAN MCARTHUR,

Via email.

Hitler   **Mr Fussy**

Sir,
Are Adolf Hitler and Mr Fussy by any chance related? I think we should be told. Do I win £10? (No, Ed.)

Yours aye,
MR I SPEND TOO MUCH TIME ON THE INTERNET,

Via email.

Skeleton   **Campbell**

Sir,
The recent heightened exposure, as it were, of the Lib Dems has reminded me of the close resemblance between Ming 'Menzies' Campbell and the jovial character who advertised Scotch videotape in the 1980s. It would be cruel to comment on the double irony of Lib Dems/skeletons and the fact that the Scotch ad carried the slogan 're-record, not fade away' to the tune of 'Not Fade Away', so I shall refrain.

Yours,
JAMIE MILNE,

Via email.

Mauresmo   **Legolas**

Sir,
Whilst watching Wimbledon I noticed a striking similarity between the women's champion, Amélie Mauresmo, and the elven archer Legolas from the Lord of the Rings trilogy. Perhaps this explains the accuracy of some of her longer-range shots?

Yours,
JEREMY WILKINSON,

Via email.

Dot   **Coco**

Sir,
I recently came across a photograph of Coco Chanel and was struck by how much she looks like Dot Branning (née Cotton) of "EastEnders". Are they related?

Yours,
GRAHAM RENNIE,

Glasgow.

Reid   **Genet**

Sir,
Has anyone noticed the resemblance between New Labour's Glaswegian hard man John "fit for purpose" Reid and the gay French novelist and playwright Jean Genet? Reid would no doubt have the jailbird Genet out of the country on the first available Eurostar.

Yours,
ADRIAN TAHOURDIN,

London SW18.

Ronaldo   **Evans**

Sir,
I'm a long-time fan of Lee Evans, with his hilarious comic routines and comic pratfalls. I was wondering if Cristiano Ronaldo was also as good at telling jokes?

Yours faithfully,
HUGH SHIPMAN,

Via email.

Sontaran

Ackroyd

Sir,
Peter Ackroyd, now presenting the Romantics BBC2 programme, seems to be a relative of the cloned warrior Sontarans, sworn enemies of Doctor Who. Does the D-G know about this?
Yours,
PETER FINDLEY,

Via email.

Haniyeh

Clooney

Sir,
You cannot have missed the extraordinary resemblance between George Clooney, spokesman for the International Terrorist Group "Hamish", and Ismail Haniyeh, the actor condemned by all civilised nations for his role in the new Hollywood blockbuster, Sorryana? Are they perhaps related?
MICHAEL KRUSE,

Nagoya, Japan.

Toynbee

Clarke

Sir,
Nicky Clarke and Polly Toynbee appear to be twins. She might have recently refused to tell the Eye how much she earns, but do you think she can afford his £425-per-cut fees?
Best wishes,
ENA B. DALES,

Via email.

Big Brother contestant

Venus

Sir,
Have any of your readers noticed the remarkable similarity between the poor woman with the deformed breasts in the Big Brother house and the Willendorf Venus. As they seem to be of a similar age it's possible they are related.

Yours,
GRAHAM McCALLUM,

Via email.

Corpse

Mrs Beckham

Sir,
I was watching Tim Burton's "Corpse Bride" last night and I noticed the startling similarity between Mrs Victoria Beckham and a corpse
Yours,
PHILIP KNIGHT,

Via email.

Schiele

Crouch

Sir,
Have you noticed the marked similarity between Croucho of the robot dance and Egon Schiele's self-portrait of 1909? There could be a copyright issue here.
JULIAN BARNES,

London NW5

Thomas

Daffyd

Sir,
The famous poet, piss artist and player of the pink oboe Dylan Thomas, has a close resemblance to The Only Gay In The Village, Daffyd. Is there any chance of them being related? (No doubt, Dylan would say Llareggub.)
Regards,
DAVE ALEXANDER,

Swansea.

Mario

Professor Winston

Sir,
I've just noticed that Professor Winston looks like Mario.
A.J. NORGATE,

Via email

Mr Potato Head

ElBaradei

Sir,
Has anyone else noticed the extraordinary resemblance between Dr Mohamed ElBaradei, head of the UN nuclear weapons inspectorate, and Mr Potato Head, from Pixar's Toy Story? Could they be in some way related? I think we should be told...
MATT BELL,

Cambridgeshire.

Wrath

Burns

Sir,
I was struck by the similarity between Mr Peter Burns (self-confessed diva) and the Wrath from Stargate Atlantis (self-confessed planet ravager). Are they perhaps related?
Yours,
HENRY SPENCE,

Via email.

Blakey

Jowell

Sir,
Is Tessa Jowell perhaps related to "Blakey" of "On The Buses"? I think she should declare it.
HUGH ALEXANDER,

Bloxham, Oxfordshire.

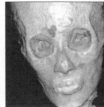
Boy King

Bill Deedes

Sir,
I was struck by the resemblance between Mr W.F. Deedes and the "Boy King" Tutankhamen. Are the two related, and could this perhaps explain the beloved scribe's longevity?
Yours sincerely,
A.J. NORGATE,

Southsea, Hants.

BBC Radio 3
90.2-92.4 FM

Composer of the Week:
Berlusconi
Opera
*The Briber of Seville
(surely "Milan"? Ed.)*

Act One Silvio, the robber baron, is about to be put on trial in the city of Milano. His wily English advocate, Davide Millsano, is worried about what he is meant to say to the judge. But Silvio puts his fears at rest by presenting him with a huge bag of gold, while singing the aria *"Donna tell the truth"*.

Act Two The advocate and his wife, Tessa Jowellina, are dining in their London mansion. She innocently inquires of her husband where all the money has come from to pay for their lavish lifestyle. He reassures her with the haunting aria *"Donna worry your pretty little head about nothing"*.

Act Three We are now back in Milan, where Millsoni is under arrest for taking a bribe from the brigand leader. He sings the aria *"Sono idiotico"*, in which he explains that, although he is innocent, he made a terrible error by accepting the gold in return for not telling the truth.

Act Four Signora Jowellina is distraught, and is summoned to explain herself to her employer, Antonio di Blairio, the chief minister of England. In his aria *"Scandalo magnato"*, he tells her that it will not look too good if her husband's conduct is reported in the newspapers. Turning this into a duet, she replies with *"Vacanza fribi"*, in which she reminds the prime minister that he is not one to talk when it comes to accepting lavish gifts from the robber baron.

Act Five The great courtroom scene, in which finally all ends happily – when it transpires that the presiding judge is Silvio's uncle. The chorus happily proclaim *"Tutti innocenti"* and all the accused leave the court as free men and are invited to a celebration banquet in the robber baron's castle, the Palazzo Corrupti.

ADVERTISEMENT

Introducing the new
TESSA ACCOUNT

AN INCREDIBLE opportunity for investors. All you have to do is sign up for a **TESSA** and you get £350,000 paid directly via a series of offshore accounts into your bank – and you get your mortgage paid off! And it's all tax-free! Your **TESSA** account is guaranteed to give you a huge return of up to £350,000 overnight and you don't have to say or do anything!

Just keep your mouth shut and watch your money grow, grow, grow!!

Apply now to Il Banco di Berlusconi, Piazza di Silenzi, Milan for the investment opportunity of a lifetime sentence *(shurely 'lifetime'? Ed)*

WARNING
With a Tessa you can go down as well as up

THE ALTERNATIVE VOICE

DEIRDRE SPART (Co-Chair of the Women's Collective Against Glass Ceilings And Pro Fair Trade In Non-Nut-Based Breakfast Cereals).

The sickening hypocrisy of the male-dominated media in attacking Ms Tessa Jowell just because she is a woman is totally sickening and totally reminiscent of the notorious witch-hunts of the Middle Ages which caused the deaths of millions and millions of innocent women just because... er... anyway why should Mrs Jowell know anything about the family finances, that is a job for a man, er, hang on... anyway, if Ms Jowell had been a man, she would have been totally exonerated and let off the hook like David Blunkett and Peter Mandelson, whereas just because she is a woman, she is... er... *(cont. p. 94)*

Jowell Cleared On All Counts – Official

THE report of an inquiry conducted by the Cabinet Secretary, Sir Gus O'Donnell, into the conduct of the Rt. Hon. Tessa Jowell MP, in relation to various huge sums of money which her husband seems to have got hold of without knowing how and without her being aware of it.

1. Terms Of Reference

I have been invited by the Prime Minister to provide an impartial report on the conduct of his great friend Mrs Jowell and to find her innocent of any malfeasance or impropriety whatsoever.

2. Evidence

I have given very careful consideration to all the evidence so far available concerning Mrs Jowell's part in this affair (i.e. yesterday's Daily Mail).

3. Assessment

It strikes me that Mrs Jowell's husband, Mr David Mills, may be a bit of a dodgy character, and is definitely not the sort of person with whom politicians of the stature of Mrs Jowell or Mr Silvio Berlusconi should be associated.

However, there is no evidence that Mrs Jowell was in any way cognisant of her husband's distinctly shady activities, and when she signed the alleged £350,000 mortgage form on her kitchen table, it now appears that she was suffering a temporary attack of amnesia caused by bird flu. It was also quite dark at the time, and the print in the contract was very small.

Mrs Jowell tells me that she had left her glasses on the hall table, on a huge pile of cash given to her husband by Signor Berlusconi. *(I am not sure that this bit should go in – what do you think? G. O'D.)*

4. Recommendations

It might be a good idea, as Mr Campbell has suggested, if Mrs Jowell were to announce that she and her husband are to effect a temporary end to their marriage, until such unfortunate events have been forgotten, and we have all moved on.

5. Conclusions

Personally, I blame the media.

(PS. I hope this is what you wanted, Tony. As you know, I had to scribble this out on the train on the way home.)

© Lord O'Donnell of Whitewash 2008.

D I A R Y

MALCOLM McLAREN *(manager, The Sex Pistols):* I followed the aesthetic legacy of William Morris and John Ruskin. Art for art's sake. Make everything beautiful, even ugliness. So when Sid sicked up onstage for the first time, I saw all the colours of the rainbow in the arc of his puke. And I thought, This Is The Future.

JOHN LYDON *(formerly Johnny Rotten):* There's lots of wankers go round claiming they was there when Sid first puked up. Well, fuck them, basically, they're fucking liars, 'cos most of them weren't.

He'd been eating this sandwich, cheese-and-tomato. With a bit of pickle. Well, quite a lot of pickle, actually.

RAT SCABIES *(former drummer with The Damned, now assistant sales manager, Rumbelows, Ipswich):* Okay, so there's a lot of debate amongst historians about that sandwich Sid puked up. Most agree on it being cheese-and-tomato, right? But it's the pickle that's the issue. I don't remember there being no pickle, and I should know. After all I skidded on that sick, and fell into it, head-first.

DAVID STARKEY *(TV historian, former bass guitarist with Sham 69):* It's not only ludicrous but frankly preposterous to claim that there was no pickle in Sidney Vicious's sandwich on that or indeed any other occasion. It was an idea first mooted by Hugh Trevor-Roper in his grotesquely over-rated history of punk, and it seems to have caught on. Hughie should have had his bottom smacked. But I was there that night and I should know. Vicious was a man addicted to pickle, and that pool of vomit was full to the brim with it. Branston's, if you really want to know.

PAUL MORLEY *(music journalist):* Pickle or no pickle, when Sid puked over that zeitgeist stage, he ultimately created a post-modernist seismic whirlpool zeitgeist of sublime yet catastrophic zeitgeist, at once strangely familiar yet completely unfamiliar, a masterpiece of vomit that both expressed the whole complex zeigeist of the times yet was ultimately destroyed by it.

MALCOLM McLAREN: I bagged up Sid's sick at the time and sold it to Nick Serota a few years back. It'll be centrepiece at a major Punk retrospective at Tate Britain in the autumn. The question is, how to hang it.

PETE SHELLEY *(former lead vocalist with The Buzzcocks, now West Midlands Area Manager, Callard and Bowser):* I was at the 100 Club when they invented pogo-ing. By the end of that Tuesday night, you had all these people jumping up and down. No-one had ever jumped up and

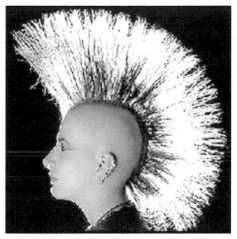

PUNK: AN ORAL HISTORY

down before ever in the history of the world. It wasn't just historic. It was, well, historic.

ANN WIDDECOMBE *(former drummer with Penetration, now Conservative MP for Maidstone and The Weald):* I was, as ever, first through the door at the 100 Club. This was before I was in a band, I was just a fan in those days. It was a Tuesday, and I was in my bondage gear, with some sort of tight PVC hood over my head. And halfway through a really super set by The Damned I just started jumping up and down in time with the movement. So I can honestly claim to have invented it. And I remember thinking, "My goodness, this is a smashing new dance! Why not let's call it the Pogo?!!" So I turned to my chums with their safety pins all neatly in place and I said, "Come on, you lot – let's pogo!" Yes, it was exhausting, but it made for very healthy exercise, too. You know, it's all too easy to forget what good exercise Punk provided.

JOHN LYDON: It wasn't The Damned playing that Tuesday, it was us. I was gobbing at the audience, and they was standing with their mouths open, pogoing up and down like penguins, trying to catch it. It was a semolina moment in the history of punk.

VIVIENNE WESTWOOD *(fashion designer):* I was hugely influenced by my reading of Thomas Hardly's novels at the time. To me, those torn T-shirts were very Jess of the D'Urbervilles. And the moment Johnny Rotten walked into the shop, I thought: Mayor of Castlebridge! So the whole

punk look was really a homage to Thomas Hardly, but before the end of that summer I had moved on to Marco Proust, who inspired the whole safety-pin look, very Recherche, very Tom Perdew.

STING *(former singer and bassist with Police):* We tried to bring something new and exciting to punk. Regular laundry, decent transport, vintage wine, that sort of thing. And I think we proved that punk could get you to places no-one expected: a stately home outside Salisbury, for instance, or a country estate in Umbria.

SIR MENZIES CAMPBELL *(former triangle player, The Clash, now leader of the Liberal Democrats):* I am of the same generation as Vivienne, and, like her, I was proud to call myself a punk in those days, oh, very much so. No, I was never sick in a concert hall, but let me add this: if I had been, I would not have been ashamed to admit it, and I would, of course, been the first to lend a hand with clearing up the vomit in question. I have always regarded the safety-pin as a precious asset in our community.

It is my aim to bring some of that very real sense of youthful energy and enthusiasm – not to mention vomit – to the Liberal Democratic Party of today. In a very real way, to be a Liberal Democrat is to be a punk, and I intend to keep it that way. I know my colleague Simon Hughes claims to have been a founder member of X-Ray Spex, and I congratulate him on his considerable achievement. My abiding memory of the punk movement? Its belief in creating a strong, effective society with a greener, fairer and more democratic Britain at peace with itself at home and admired abroad.

MALCOLM McLAREN: After inventing punk, I soon got bored with it, so I went on to invent modern opera, then colour photography, then compact discs, and, more recently, the i-Pod. Now, when I play golf at Wentworth with Johnny Rotten, we don't give a fuck – we sometimes leave our top buttons undone! We're still rebels, see. Yeah!

A. S. BYATT *(former bassist with The Slits, now author and critic):* In a very real sense, the punk movement has had an extraordinarily symbiotic effect on the great narrative adventure that is, in a very real sense, the modern novel. By which I mean that in a very profound sense that we are all in what I would call the post-punk period, by which I mean – I'm sorry, you'll have to excuse me because, in a very real sense, I feel a vomit coming on.

As told to
C R A I G   B R O W N

"I see the Valkyries have 'pimped' their rides"

GREEN AWARDS HIMSELF A £1.2bn BONUS

GENGHIS KHAN 'UNSURE ABOUT DAVID CAMERON'

by Our Political Staff **Matthew D'Anconservative**

THE RIGHT-WING elder statesman Lord Genghis of Khan has expressed doubts about the direction that the Conservative Party is taking under its new leader, David Cameron.

In an address to the influential 1222 Committee, Lord Genghis told members: "It is all very well trying to move the Party to the centre ground but if you lose the traditional core support on the right then you will never achieve what you want to do, i.e. vanquish your enemies, chase them before you, rob them of their wealth, see those dear to them bathed in tears, or clasp to your bosom their wives and daughters."

He then added, "Though I suppose we might pick up a few Lib Dem votes along the way."

David Cameron, however, was unmoved by this unprovoked attack by Lord Genghis.

Mongolia-Than-Thou

"Whilst I am grateful for the advice of the eminent former Tory statesman," he said, "I do think we have to try to create a more modern and inclusive Party, one that is keener on social equality and less keen on sweeping through the world putting opponents to the sword and burning their villages."

Lord Genghis of Khan is 800 years old.

BECKHAMS STILL HAPPY

We've dropped the libel case

Makes a change from your trousers, David

HERE'S £20M. NOW FIND OUT WHY EVERYONE HATES US

Image Consultants

CHELSEA

BESTIE

That Premiership Football Team in Full

CHEAT			
DIVER	FAKER	ACTOR	SCAMMER
BOGUS	FRAUD	CON	SHAM
	OUCH	AARGH	

MANAGER: WHINGER

CHERIE'S HUMAN RIGHTS SPEECH

It'll cost you an arm and a leg

I like the sound of that

THE TIMES

She's back and she's cleverer than ever

Mary Ann Bighead on what I did on my holidays

WHO would have thought it? Four months, 40,000 miles, and 400,000 words later the Bighead family has returned to these shores, weary, suntanned, but above all very, very clever.

Yes, there were some bad moments in our round the world trip. Brainella (3) nearly lost her copy of Proust in a cafe, which would have spelt disaster for her attempts to translate it into classical Persian. Then there was the time when Intelligencia (7) fell ill in the ancient Venezuela town of Hiyi Quw. Luckily her advanced medical physiology PhD allowed her to diagnose herself with a rare tropical complaint before the local doctor (Dr Haus) could even begin to solve the mystery.

But on the whole the Bigheads triumphed in adversity! Have you sailed a dug-out canoe over a waterfall and into a volcano? We have. Have you explained Einstein's relativity theory to Mayan priests at the top of the Pyramid of Smahtipantza? We have. Have you found a cure for cancer? OK, we didn't, but then we only had four months!

But seriously, every family in Britain should go on a trip like this. Even if they aren't very rich and they haven't got a job at the Times waiting when they get back. Because it is an experience of a lifetime, which we have done and you haven't.

So, I know you are all dying to know the answer to the question, "What did you learn, Mary Ann, from your amazing adventure?" The answer is not very much because I knew it all already! They say travel broadens the mind but then in the Bighead family that might not be possible!

© Mary Ann Bighead

MURRAY SET TO REPLACE HENMAN

by Our Tennis Staff **Lunchtime O'verhype**

ANDY MURRAY, the teenage tennis sensation, is about to become the new Tim Henman, according to Britain's tennis pundits.

"Murray has got what it takes," said one. "He can do quite well in minor championships, get our hopes up and then fail to win Wimbledon – just like Tim."

Said another, "He's the perfect man on whom to place our unrealistic expectations.

"He's got everything we want from a British tennis player. He's got some good ground strokes, a fruity girlfriend and no chance of beating Federer.

Come on, Andy!

"So we can build him up in the next few months and then lay into him over the summer." Andy Murray is 11.

POLICE LOG

Neasden Central Police Station
Office hours: 9-12 Mon-Tues (except Tuesday)

1100 hrs All officers reported to canteen for debriefing on 'Operation Gorilla', to apprehend the fur coat allegedly worn by celebrity transsexual Miss Peter Burns. Several officers had been deployed to keep a close watch on the station television screen to ensure that the aforesaid garment, manufactured in breach of the Import of Endangered Primates Directive, 2003/64/EC, did not leave the premises of the so-called 'Big Brother House'. When these officers suspected that a serious crime had been committed, reinforcements were called in at 2.49 a.m. and 25 officers (including 8 WPCs and the Firearms Unit) were despatched to apprehend the coat and charge Ms Burns with first-degree murder of an unknown creature of simian orientation. Sadly the officers were denied access by a security guard, in accordance with the Data Protection Act 1998, and were forced to regroup in the adjoining Star of Saddam oriental restaurant across the road. While continuing their surveillance, they consumed the following items: 32 plates of prawn vindaloo with rice and chips and 72 pints of King Cobra lager (except for PC Onanugu, our designated driver).

1233 hrs An emergency response team was summoned to attend a serious mushroom-picking incident at the Neasden Recreation Ground. A white female of middle-age, later identified as Mrs Ludmilla Fearnley-Whittingstall, had been spotted by Community Support Officer Blears engaged in the act of the illegal removal of fungoid substances from a grass verge adjacent to the paddling pool, in direct contravention of Section 81 of the Indigenous Mushroom, Puffball and Other Fungi (Protection) Regulations 2003. An armed response unit, including bomb disposal experts and a trained interpreter, WPC Alibhai-Brown, was sent to arrest and/ or terminate the suspect, by lethal force if necessary. Mrs Fearnley-Whittingstall offered no resistance, but unfortunately a number of toddlers in the pool were caught in the cross-fire.

1555 hrs A complaint was received from a member of the public concerning a serious incident of racism committed by Ms Claire Squeakey, presenter of the 'Neasden Drive Time Show', who was alleged to have said 'Funny lot, the Welsh'. Ten officers from the Anti-Racism and Xenophobia Unit attended the offices of Radio Neasden FM and stormed Studio 1B, using stun grenades, water cannon and sniffer dogs. It transpired that Ms Squeaky was no longer on the premises because she had "gone to her Pilates class". The officers then interrogated the studio manager, Mr Terry Barcode, who under intensive questioning admitted to having been responsible for the death of the late Diana, Princess of Wales. He was let off with a caution and was admitted to hospital with severe internal injuries.

2215 hrs Message received regarding the outbreak of gang warfare on Mary Seacoal Street (formerly Florence Nightingale Avenue) outside the police station involving some 30 Somali and other East African youths engaged in a 'turf battle' over the right to sell crack cocaine in the vicinity of the bus shelter. The caller was invited, to ring back after 9 a.m. the following morning by means of a recorded announcement, which also advised the caller that any further attempts to contact the station would result in a prosecution for the wasting of police time.

That Goldsmith/ Knacker Illegal Taped Conversation In Full

Knacker: Hello, hello, hello, Knacker of the Yard here.

Lord Goldsmith: It's the Attorney General. I want to talk to you about phone tapping.

Knacker: Can you just say that again for level?

Goldsmith: Look, we're not happy about you going round bugging anyone you feel like.

Knacker: Hang on. I think I've pressed the wrong button. Testing! Testing! 1-2-3...

Goldsmith: What?

Knacker: What did you have for breakfast?

Goldsmith: You have no right to ask that. You are invading my privacy. I demand to see my Solicitor General.

Knacker: Oh, I see what's gone wrong. I haven't put a tape in *(cont p. 94)*

"It's Icarus – I think he's contracted Avian Flu"

47

REID DENIES ARMY CUTS HAVE GONE TOO FAR

"Also, Herman, it forces enemy cartoonists to use more of their precious Indian ink"

CHURCH TO STAR IN ADVERT

I'm the new stuff-your-face of Walkers Crisps

'WE'RE NOT GOING TO CUT AND RUN'
Reid Spells It Out

by Our Political Staff **Lunchtime O'Bore**

"WE'RE not going to cut and run." That was the clear message spelled out today by Defence Secretary Dr John Reid, as he outlined the government's plans to withdraw troops from Iraq as soon as possible.

"We're going to see the job through," he pledged, "and as soon as the job is through, then will be the time to implement our two-part strategy, first to cut, and then, at the appropriate time, to run."

Reid My Lips

But Dr Reid denied that the British Government would set the timetable for the orderly cutting and running of British troops.

"The responsibility for that lies firmly and squarely with the Iraqi government," he said, "as soon as there is one.

"Only when we tell them to ask us to leave will we begin the countdown to the process of cutting and running. And as long as the Americans agree, that is when we will implement Operation Dunkirk."

STOP PRESS

■ **Reid Orders Remainder of British Army Into Afghan Danger Zone** – "Operation 'Charge of Light Brigade' vital to future of Afghan democracy," says no one.

That Official Consent Form In Full

I, [⬚⬚⬚⬚⬚⬚⬚⬚⬚⬚] *(here fill in name, eg, Chantelle, Waynetta, Janinda etc)*, being of sound mind, having consumed not more than the following quantities of alcoholic beverage in the previous hour:

● 6 Bacardi Breezers
● 8 Vodka and Red Bulls
● 12 pints XXXX lager
● 15 pints Strongbow Cider
● 1 bottle of Meths
● 2 boxes Napa Valley Shiraz (min. contents 8 litres)
● 1 bottle Babycham

and, thereby, for all official and legal purposes, being below the insobriety threshold, do hereby give full consent and immunity from prosecution to [⬚⬚⬚⬚⬚⬚⬚⬚⬚] *(here fill in name of prospective sexual partner, eg Wayne, Shane, Vijay, Sir Peregrine Worsthorne, etc.)* to hereinafter engage in any of the following activities, namely:

● Pilates
● Aerlingus
● Rastafarianism
● Parcelforce
● Brokeback Mountain

Copies of this form can be downloaded from the internet at your primary school from www.safeshag.condom

---

GLENDA SLAGG

FLEET STREET'S SUPERBUG!! SHE'LL GET YOU IN THE END!!

■ NOW I"VE heard it all!!?! Mrs Oaten is taking back her good-for-nothing pervy hubby into the bosom of her home!?!?? Urghhh!! You have my permission to be sick!?!! What do you have to do nowadays to get kicked out on your B-U-M??!? (Except in Mr Oaten's case he'd probably enjoy that?!??) For gawd's sake Mrs O – wise up!!?! Change the locks, throw out his suitcases, and buy a Rottweiler!?! Before you wake up with the whole of Soho sharing your nuptial bed!?!!

■ HATS OFF TO MRS OATEN?!? She's the Lib Dem MP's missus who's found it in her heart to say, "Welcome home, hubby – let's forget about your sleazy nights of shame and the three-in-a-bed sex romps with rent boys"!!?! Bless!?! Your unselfish action shines like a beacon to us all in this age of easy judgements and all too ready condemnation of pervy husbands who go off and commit disgusting acts with randy rent boys!?!?

■ DIDN'T YOU weep when you saw *Brokeback Mountain*, Mister?!? The touching tale of two lovelorn gay guys finding solace in the sheep-strewn sunsets of Wyoming!?!! I know a tear trickled down my cheek as the credits rolled!?! Cowboy hats off to a movie that tells the story of a love that dare not speak its name!?!! At last, thank Gawd, we've grown up enough to watch an adult movie without sniggering about what other gay westerns might have been called!?!

■ *HERE they are – Auntie Glenda's Gay Cowboy films in full:*
● **High Camp**
● **Once Upon A Time In A Vest**
● **Lovers' Tiff at the OK Corral**
● **Well Hung 'Em High**
● **Dances With Wooves**
● **Butch Cassidy And The Sun Bed Kid**
● **She Wore A Pink Ribbon**
● **A Fisting Of Dollars**
(You're fired. Ed.)

Byeeee!!!

48

LOVE ON THE NILE

By Dame Sylvie Krin

THE STORY SO FAR: Charles and Camilla are making a visit to the mysterious and ancient land of Egypt. Now read on...

 "IT's incredible to think that those Pharaoh chaps could do all this thousands of years ago."

Charles, in a Merchant and Ivory panama hat, waved his pencil in the direction of the unmistakable towering mass of the Great Pyramid of Cheops.

The midday sun was blazing down mercilessly on the royal party, as the prince sat at his easel, trying to capture the tricky outlines of the last surviving wonder of the ancient world.

"I mean, those kings were allowed to rule for thousands of years, without people constantly criticising them and publishing all their diaries and so forth."

As Camilla wilted in the heat, trying to cool herself with a traditional glass of chilled Fruit 'n' Khamun herbal tea (which, according to the label, had been "drunk by the pharaohs since time began"), she scarcely had the energy to reply. "Yes, Chazza. Can we go back to the hotel now? It's bloody hot."

Charles shook his head, and dipped his brush again in the yellow ochre. "Hang on, old thing, I've just got to get this pyramid-thingie right, but that camel keeps getting in the way."

Indeed, at that moment, a swarthy *fellahmalad*, or local tribesman, tugging his reluctant camel behind him, approached the prince, with his hand stretched out in expectation.

"You paint my picture, Effendi, you pay me 80 dollars, or the curse of Allah will be upon you."

"No, no," remonstrated the prince. "I'm all in favour of this Allah chap. That's why I'm here – to build bridges between our two great faiths."

The camel-minder was, however, unmoved by the prince's plea.

"Ok, you no give me money. I take woman instead."

At this point Camilla had had enough.

"Stuff this for a game of soldiers, Chazza. You can shoot the breeze with Johnny-Arab here. I'm going back for a shower and a lie-down."

As a squad of highly-armed tourist police materialised from behind the nearby Sphinx to escort the hapless camel-owner into the Nile, Charles was left alone to complete his emergent masterpiece, which he had already provisionally entitled *"Study Of Pyramid and Camel by His Royal Highness the Prince of Wales"*.

But as the midday heat became ever more oppressive, the royal artist found his eyelids growing heavy and a darkness seemed to descend on the land...

 SOMEHOW Charles seemed to see before him a scene of extraordinary activity as thousands of semi-naked slaves toiled in the desert to raise a pyramid larger than any that had been seen before.

It was he, he knew, who had designed the whole thing as a monument to his lifelong love of architecture.

And there were his plans, etched on

the sheet of papyrus, with a series of hieroglyphs proclaiming it as "The Great Pyramid of Chazza", in the Valley of the Nearly-Kings.

What a moment this was, when the vision he had nurtured over millennia was finally coming to fruition, despite all the ill-informed criticism from jealous scribes and petty bureaucrats. Not to mention the scorn of his aged mother, the great Queen Neferdie, who had already ruled for 800 years, and who, some said, had doomed all his efforts with the so-called "Curse of the Mummy".

This would show the world, he thought, "Look upon my works, ye mighty despair sort-of-thingie," he declaimed to the sweating masses to whom he had given employment under his imaginative and so little-appreciated Pharaoh's Trust scheme, where the young people of Egypt could learn to use traditional vernacular materials to create the world's first fully-organic pyramid.

But what was this cloud of dust approaching him across the desert sands?

It was a messenger on a camel. As he drew nearer, Charles recognised the familiar features of the Egyptian carpet-seller Mohamed Al Fayed, who had earlier offered him his entire stock in return for a passport.

"Fuggin' bad news, oh great one," declared the newly-arrived messenger. "It's official. The Princess Diana, your beautiful bride, *was* killed in a chariot accident. And it's all your fault. As exclusively revealed by me in the *Niley Express*, it was you and your father, Philip of Macedonia, the wily Greek naval commander, to blame."

Charles clutched his head in despair. This story he was dreaming seemed strangely familiar.

But even worse was to come. The dusky merchant smiled as he explained that, by popular decree, the new pyramid was to be demolished and replaced by a giant water feature, to be known as "The Diana Memorial Fountain (closed for repair)".

And, as if by magic, the pyramid vanished before his eyes, to be replaced by an immense circular trench, with the entire River Nile flowing through it, while thousands of workers joyfully shouted "Great is Diana of the Egyptians. All hail to Her Highness..."

 "HIGHNESS... Highness... Your Highness. It's time to go." The voice of Sir Alan Fitztightly broke in on Charles's reverie.

"They're all waiting in the Great Hall of the ancient Islamic University of Al Ahn Qu'ran to give you your honorary degree."

"Is that for my pyramid?" Charles asked, as he emerged from his now fast-fading dream of greatness.

"Do you know, Fitztightly, they're actually putting a fountain where my pyramid used to be. It really is appalling."

"Indeed, sire, but we really must get you out of this heat..."

(To be continued)

© *Sylvie Krin, from the Swan-Hellenic Nile Cruise Collection 2006.*

CHAI PATEL ADMITTED TO PRIORY

by Our Medical Staff **Dr Thomas Utterfraud**

ONE of Labour's top donors, Dr Chai Patel, has been admitted to his own clinic suffering from acute depression brought on by a lack of peerage.

Doctors who have examined Dr Patel confirm that he is a victim of Crony's Disease. What happens, says a doctor, is that the patient donates a large sum of money to the Labour Party in the expectation that he will be cured of being a commoner and will be admitted immediately to the House of Lords.

Donor Kebabed

In very rare cases, however, such as Dr Patel's, the donated money is taken by open wallet surgery, but the host body (in this case, the Labour Party) then rejects the donor.

This can result in feelings of anger, depression, hurt feelings, lack of esteem and a strong desire to give interviews to the Daily Mail attacking the government.

● *Read Dr Utterfraud's blog on utterfraud.blog.com*

"Luckily for us the serpent pointed out that without a styrofoam container of coffee in our hands we'd be walking around stark naked"

ONLY IN THE DAILY EXPRESS

Was Nessie Really Princess Diana?

SENSATIONAL new evidence today has revealed that the Loch Ness Monster was in fact Princess Diana swimming.

The so-called "trunk" that was visible on the surface of the Loch was, in fact, our beloved Princess Diana's arm, as she waved desperately to people on the shore, trying to attract their attention before she was kidnapped by the Duke of Edinburgh's personal submarine and *(cont. p. 94)*

THAT GALLOWAY RADIO PHONE-IN SHOW
What You WIll MIss

George Galloway: And our next caller is Saddam from Baghdad. Hello, Saddam. What is your point?

Saddam Hussein *(for it is he)*: Hello, George – alright?

George Galloway: Yes, I'm alright, thanks. We're talking about Milosevic here.

Saddam: Well, it's obvious he was poisoned, isn't it? Do you think I should eat anything while I'm in jail? Because, I mean, they could easily do me in too, couldn't they, George? I mean, I wouldn't even know, would I?

George Galloway: Good point, Saddam.

Saddam: And, what's more, mate, I'm *innocent*, George.

Galloway: I know that – we all know that – and, if it were up to me, Saddam, I'd open up the jail and say, "You're free, mate, it's President Bush who should be locked up for war crimes".

Saddam: Too right, George. Anyway, I've gotta say, I love the show.

Galloway: Cheers, and I salute your courage and indefatigability. And our next caller is Osama from Afghanistan who wants to talk about the rugby.

Osama: I mean, England were rubbish, George, let's face it, but that Italian side, they could be World Champions in a few years, couldn't they? *(continues all night)*

Publishing Sensation as New Mr Men Launched

by our Literary Staff **Phil Boots**

THE WORLD of children's books was rocked to its foundations by the announcement that a new series of Mr Men charcters had been created to join the old family favourites such as **Mr Happy**, **Mr Nosey** and **Little Miss Naughty**.

The new characters, unveiled to gasps of admiration from the world's media, include:

Mr Easy-to-Draw

Mr Money-for-Old-Rope

Little Miss No-Opportunity-to-Cash-In

(That's enough new characters, Ed.)

Said publisher **Mr Greedy,** "This new series is sure to bring a smile to our little accountant's face."

Apparently
BY MIKE BARFIELD

PARTY LEADERS AND THEIR BIKES

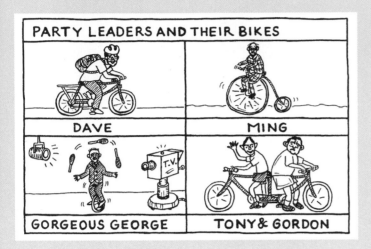

DAVE — MING — GORGEOUS GEORGE — TONY & GORDON

WERTHER'S: THE COMPLETE CONFECTIONERY

ORIGINAL — AUTHORISED COPY — DE LUXE COLLECTORS' EDITION — OBVIOUS FAKE

ebay™ SWEETS current bid: £3·10

AUTUMN: AN HSE GUIDE

GLOVES MUST BE WORN — EYE PROTECTION MANDATORY — TOXIC — HIGH VISIBILITY VESTS NEEDED — FALL! — SAFETY HELMETS COMPULSORY — FIRE RISK — MAY CONTAIN NUTS — BIOHAZARD — MIST

ESKIMO WORDS FOR SNOW: A PROPHETIC GUIDE

VANNISHTT — MELTID — ORLTHORD — GORNN — DIFROSHTID — TOATLI BUGURD

JAIL BIRDS: THE ONES YOU REALLY MUST WATCH

HOODED CROW — CHAVFINCH — CRACK HOUSE MARTIN — TAGTAIL — HEROIN GULL — ASBOCET

CHILDREN'S HAND GAMES: HOW THEY DEVELOPED

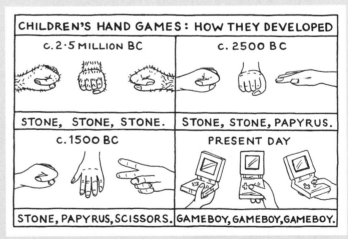

c. 2·5 MILLION BC — STONE, STONE, STONE.
c. 2500 BC — STONE, STONE, PAPYRUS.
c. 1500 BC — STONE, PAPYRUS, SCISSORS.
PRESENT DAY — GAMEBOY, GAMEBOY, GAMEBOY.

ANT AND DEC: THEIR 'POKER FACES'

SAME TOP CASH PRIZE AS 'MILLIONAIRE'... — SAME MUSIC AND LOOK AS 'WEAKEST LINK'... — SAME ELIMINATION CHATS WITH CONTESTANTS, TOO... — TIME FOR ANOTHER VISIT TO THE BANK...

WHEN LIGHTS GO WRONG: A SEASONAL WARNING

WISH! AVE MARIA NOEL! SANTA FROSTIE! — I H AVE NO TA STE

DAY TIME — NIGHT TIME

Norman Kember

THE NAIVE IDIOT WHO WENT TO IRAQ

by Our Defence Staff BAZRA BAGHDADIBOY

HE WAS told not to go, but he defied his friends and advisers and went anyway. He claimed to have a mission to bring peace to the troubled land of Iraq. He even claimed that God had told him to go.

But of course the inevitable happened. He immediately got into trouble and Iraqi militants targeted his peace mission.

Shocking And Awful

Army generals were particularly scathing about what they called "this reckless and silly adventure".

Said Sir Michael Jackson, "We in the armed forces have better things to do than rescue some foolhardy idealist who brings disaster on himself."

The General continued: "And he's not even grateful. The taxpayer has spent millions of pounds trying to extricate this deluded fool from Iraq and he doesn't even say thank you."

However, the man at the centre of the storm remains unrepentant. "I would go in again," said Tony Blair. "I have a deep faith in myself and I believe that war is the only solution to the problems of peace-torn Iraq."

Norman Kember is 94.

LABOUR TREASURER 'KEPT IN THE DARK' SHOCK

by Our Political Staff Phil Coffers

THE MAN at the centre of the Peers-For-Loans row, Mr Jack Dromey, today claimed that key information was denied him during the whole affair.

"For a start," he told reporters, "I had no idea that I was Treasurer of the Labour Party. I was under the impression that I was working for a political organisation committed to wholesale privatisation, American defence policy and personal enrichment.

"Imagine my anger," he continued, "when I discovered that this was actually the Labour Party.

"Next thing they'll be telling me I'm married to Harriet Harman." *(cont. p. 94)*

New Words

Loan *(noun)*: A gift of money, usually for political purposes, which does not have to be given back. Example: "Thank you for your very generous loan. Your peerage is in the post" *(letter from T. Blair to an unidentified entrepreneur, 2005).*

Parole *(noun and verb)*: System whereby dangerous criminal is released from prison so that he can re-offend as often as he likes. Example: "It was unbelievable – the murderer in this case wasn't on parole" *(Court proceedings, 2006).*

Life *(noun)*: Period of time uniquely used by judicial officials – about two weeks *(see above).*

Tory *(noun)*: Political term used to describe supporter of the Labour Party. Example: "Of course he's a staunch Tory – he's in favour of high taxes and against grammar schools" *(Daily Telegraph, 2006).*

IRAN DENIES HOLOCAUST

WATER COMPANIES FEAR 'EXCUSES ARE DRYING UP'

by Our Science Editor Jonathan Leak

THE major water companies were warning customers last night that they faced "a major shortage of excuses" in the coming months.

In an official statement issued by the big waterless companies, they admit, "We face an unprecedented drought of credible reasons why we have failed to do the job we are paid to do.

No Way Hose Pipe

"For too long we have been spraying around excuses, like seasonal variation, global warming and customers wanting to use water all the time."

A spokesman confirmed that in the near future the companies would be so barren of excuses that they would have to resort to drastic measures, ie telling the truth.

"If it comes to it," said a spokesman, "we're going to put a nationwide ban on using excuses and admit that we've got leaky old pipes, we've sold off the reservoirs to housing developers and we've failed to invest in logistical systems to transport water from one area to another."

SOMETHING SCIENTISTS TOLD YOU WAS BAD FOR YOU, IS IN FACT GOOD FOR YOU

by Our Health Staff Hugh Nose

SCIENTISTS have today revealed that something that was previously thought to be bad for you is, in fact, good for you.

On Other Pages ● Something that was thought to be good for you is, in fact, bad for you ● Something that was thought to be bad for you that was revealed to be good for you is actually revealed to be bad for you.

FORBIDDEN IMAGE 'DEEPLY OFFENSIVE TO BELIEVERS'

by Our Religious Staff **Dan Ishcartoon**

THERE were violent protests last night over the suggestion that an image of Mazher Mahmood, the beloved journalist, was going to appear in a British newspaper.

Mahmood, who is worshipped by millions of "haqs" all over the world, is traditionally *never* depicted in print and to do so is seen as a crime worthy of death.

Huge Profit

Although Mahmood has occasionally been pictured wearing Arab robes and sunglasses – usually standing on the deck of a yacht or in a five-star hotel suite – his actual face is always obscured out of respect.

But now fanatical *News of the World* lawyers have taken to the streets carrying banners which read "Praise Be To Mahmood!", "Death To Galloway!" and "Behead The Enemies Of Murdoch!"

Fatwad of Cash

Advocates of free speech were, however, incensed by what

they saw as "censorship". Said Professor Greenslade, Reader in Media Studies at the Rusbridger University (formerly Toynbee Poly): "This is just special pleading on behalf of a minority group. We have the right to see what Mahmood looks like."

He continued: "We're not suggesting that he is a sleazy agent provocateur who stitches people up in order to sell newspapers – although he is."

CAMILLA'S WOMEN'S INSTITUTE JAM RECIPE

1. Tell Cook to make some jam.
2. Er...
3. That's it.

NEXT WEEK
Camilla's recipe for a State Banquet
for 250 people.

"Ohmigod! She just said her first 'Ohmigod'!"

BLAIRS ATTEND THATCHER'S 80th PARTY

It's full of ghastly old right wingers

Speak for yourself

THE DUCHESS OF CORNWALL
An Apology

IN RECENT YEARS, in common with all other newspapers, we may have given the impression that Camilla Parker-Bowles, now the Duchess of Cornwall, was a frumpy, ill-dressed, socially awkward divorcée, who was totally unsuited in every way for her future role as Queen of England. Headlines such as "Blimey, What An Old Bag?", "Hey, look What The Cat's Dragged In" or "On Yer Bike, Granny, You've Got A Face Like A Horse And We Hate You" may have reinforced the view that we in some way wished to disparage Her Royal Highness, the Duchess of Cornwall, and to compare her unfavourably with her predecessor, Diana, the Princess of Wales.

We now accept that, following her triumphant tour of the Middle East, there was not a jot or scintilla of truth in any of the above opprobrious nonsense, based as it was on no more than malicious and unsubstantiated tittle-tattle, and that, contrary to our previous allegations, Camilla is in fact the most beautiful, fashionable, stylish, witty, warm-hearted paragon of all the feminine virtues that the world has ever had the good fortune to see. She is furthermore uniquely well-equipped in every way to support the Prince in his role both as heir to the throne and future King. She is indeed the 'Queen of all our Hearts', unlike that neurotic, bulimic, stick-thin basket-case Diana who we always hated. The Eye says 'God bless you Ma'am, May you reign over us for a Cam-million years!'

NEW CAMILLA PICTURE

THOUSANDS OF MUSLIMS DON'T PROTEST SHOCK

by Our Religious Staff

AN ENORMOUS demonstration did not take place today in Trafalgar Square, as thousands of British Muslims did not protest angrily in the streets at the blowing up of a sacred mosque in Samarra in Iraq.

Not carrying placards saying, "Death to the Bombers", "Behead the Criminals" and "Massacre the Sacriligious", large numbers of Muslims did not leave their homes at all.

Said one protestor who was not there, "This appalling action offended me so deeply that I stayed in and watched television *(cont. p. 94)*

Unfunny but accurate cartoon

MAN ON TELEVISION TO MOVE TO ANOTHER CHANNEL

by Our Media Staff
Paul O'Greedy

A MAN on one television channel has moved to another. The man is to be paid more money by the channel he has moved to than the one he was on before. *(Reuters)*

Pictures, analysis, full story 1-94

Pictures, analysis, full story 1-94

POLLY FILLER

And Tribulations Of Modern Motherhood" and *"It's All Gone Au-Pair-Shaped! The Pitfalls And Prattfalls Of 21st Century Childcare"* (all published by Johnson and Pearson, now available as a 3 for 2 offer at Waterstone's).

I'M sorry, but I just don't buy this stuff about equal pay for women. How's this for a radical idea? Equal pay for men. Particularly for useless partners who live off their talented "other halves" whilst lying around watching *Pimp My Tank* live from Baghdad, presented by Peaches Geldof and Kelly Osborne on MTV Living Plus Gold all day!

The real money in this house comes from – guess who? – the woman in the equation, who is slaving away, writing best-sellers about modern motherhood, such as *"Pun In The Oven! The Pregnancy Diaries!"*, *"Yummy Money! The Trials*

THE day that Simon gets equal pay to yours truly will presumably be the same day he works out where the washing machine is, helps toddler Charlie with his saxophone practice, rustles up a gourmet meal and then does the washing up – ie, never!

I'm all for equal pay between the sexes and, unlike most people, I'm putting it into practice. That's why our new male au-pair, Yurt, from Ulan Baatar, will be getting exactly the same wage as we paid the hopeless Hasha from Northern Afghanistan, who decided that she would rather work in her warlord uncle's poppy fields than potty train toddler Charlie! Yes, he'll be getting nothing too, except of course the unique opportunity to live in a cultured, civilised, erudite, North London home with a delightful family, an iron and a big pile of underwear!! That's what *I* call equality!

© *Polly Filler 2006.*

 FEATURING **BORIS THE MENACE**
Introducing Anna the Minx!

POT CALLS KETTLE 'CHAMELEON'

by Our Political Staff **Alastair Chamebelleon** and **Boy George Osborne**

MR Tony Pot today attacked Mr David Kettle for "changing colour" in the hope of becoming more popular.

"Kettle," he said, "will do anything to please the voters. He started off as copper and has now turned completely black.

"How unlike myself," he continued, "who has always been true black and was never any other colour at all."

Cartoony Blair

Commentators said that Mr Pot's performance marked a new low in British politics. Said one, "For Mr Pot to call Mr Kettle black is a case of the Blair calling the Cameron a chameleon".

HEWITT'S 'DIGNITY NURSES' Their Role In Full

❶ To ensure that all tiresome old people will be treated with dignity, despite their being awkward, deaf, incontinent and probably ill.

❷ This duty will be carried out by a designated "dignity nurse", whose task will be to explain to the old people (by shouting in their good ear if they have one) that there are no beds (because they are full of tiresome old people like them) and that the sooner they go home to die in dignity the better it will be for everyone.

❸ If the tiresome old people insist on staying in hospital, despite all the advice they have been given by the dignity nurse, they are to be informed that the hospital has unfortunately been earmarked for closure due to the Chancellor's massive investment in the NHS.

❹ Er...

❺ That's it.

AUVERTISEMENT

THE DA *N* CONA CODE

THE world's oldest mystery is at last revealed!

How did Matthew D'Ancona become the editor of The Spectator?

Is he a member of the Secret Order of Knights of the Holy Brillo, which gives its members jobs because they take a vow of boredom?

What was the part played in this extraordinary story by Boris of Legovia and the mysterious Knights of Barclay, two brothers who lived in an impenetrable fortress on the tiny remote island of Brellu?

And was this the key to that other mystery which has baffled scholars for hundreds of years — how did the sinister Greek convict Taki Takalotofcokupthenos somehow hang onto his job?

What terrible secret did he know about D'Ancona?

Will anyone break the code?

Does anyone care?

Mush!

And that's just his policies

Let's Parlez Anglais!

by Kilometres Kingtonne

Part 94 Dans Le EU

French Delegate: Ladies and gentlemen, may I begin my remarks by...

Monsieur Chirac: Pourquoi parlez-vous anglais?

French Delegate: Because English is now the universal language of the business community...

Monsieur Chirac: Sacre bleu! Zut alors! Merde! Espèce de cochon!

French Delegate: I'm afraid I can't understand a word you are saying old boy, eh what?

(Exit Chirac dans un grand bate)

To be continued...

"We're just going to have to learn to take off another jumper, that's all"

POLICE LOG

Neasden Central Police Station
Office hours: 9-12 Mon-Tues (except Tuesday)

1100 hrs Officers called to scene of alleged armed robbery at the HSBC branch in Dinsdale Road. Officers apprehended two suspects carrying shotguns and bags containing £100,000 in cash. In accordance with the new Crime Reduction guidelines, the two armed criminals were given a caution before they were allowed to proceed on their way to the airport. Due to this delay, PCs Clapham and Stockwell assisted them on their outward journey to Colombia by driving them to Heathrow Terminal Five.

1130 hrs An armed response team was sent to Dinsdale Road to arrest the assistant manager of the HSBC, Mr Vijay Sunblest, who had earlier reported an alleged armed robbery at his bank premises. After a short gun battle in which Mr Sunblest was unfortunately fatally wounded, he was posthumously arrested and charged with the offence of wasting police time.

1200 hrs 12-man S.W.A.T. Team dispatched to Herbert Morrison Comprehensive Nursery School following report of racism in playground. Officers arrest 6-year-old (name withheld for legal reasons – Wayne Nuggets, Flat 14b Etherington Estate, Neasden) for claiming franco-ethnic footballing role model Didier Drogba was "a cheat". Child was slightly seriously injured when hurling himself against officer's truncheon during struggle resisting arrest but later successfully charged with racist hate crime under Terrorism Act 2006. Officers Hainault and Uxbridge commended for bravery award.

1300 hrs Lunch break. Mrs O'Done, a senior catering assistant in the station canteen, was observed to have committed another racist hate crime by offering as the "daily special" Welsh Rarebit, in contravention of the 1986 Public Order Act, as amended in 2001 and 2003. After a brief interview with 20 officers in the holding cells, Mrs O'Done confessed to "deliberately holding up the Celtic ethnic minority to obloquy and contempt, thus inciting my customers to acts inimical to racial harmony". Mrs O'Done was later admitted to Neasden General Hospital, suffering from a self-inflicted fracture of the spine.

1500 hrs Acting on a tip-off from Community Support Officer Deirdre Dripstone, officers in squad cars were called to the Easybuy Arcade where a suspected terrorist had been seen acting suspiciously. After a high-speed chase, which resulted in only three civilian casualties, officers apprehended Mrs June Taplow, 72, under the Terrorism, Religious and Animal Rights Extremists Act 2006, for being in possession of a suspicious metal tin, carrying the label "Save The Squirrel". After a controlled explosion of the tin, Mrs Taplow was charged and remanded in Belmarsh as a "Class A" prisoner.

LAUNCH OF NEW KIDS' PAPER

Is this a dummy?

No, it's a moron

'NO CIVIL WAR'
Straw's Shock Claim

by Our Man Not In Baghdad

IRAQI leaders were stunned last night at UK Foreign Secretary Jack Straw's claim that there was "no civil war in the Labour Party".

"How can he say this," asked one, "when we see daily news footage of running battles between the two factions? The Brunnis and the Blairites are obviously attacking each other indiscriminately."

However, Mr Straw insisted that hostilities were limited to a tiny area of Downing Street and that the vast majority of the Labour Party was peaceful.

"Democracy is coming back to the Labour Party slowly," he claimed, after visiting the war zone for five minutes. "I have spoken to at least one taxi driver who works in Downing Street and he is optimistic about the future."

On Other Pages

Brown bombshell **2**
Milburn suicide **3**
Labour Party burns **4**

MODERN NURSERY RHYMES

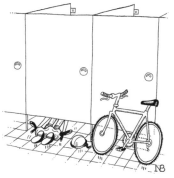

Oh dear, what can the
            matter be?
Boris got caught with
            Anna Fazackerley.
They were at it from
            Monday to Saturday.
His wife didn't know he
            was there.

(Traditional)

Product Recall UKIP

As a precautionary measure, we are recalling the following product – **The UK Independence Party** – because it has been found to contain nuts. We apologise for any inconvenience this may have caused to our voters.

How you can save the planet the Cameron way

Hi,

I'm Dave Cameron. You may have heard of me! I'm the Blue Guy who's gone Green!

Clever, eh?

But, hey guys, you can do it too, and help save the planet!

Who says it isn't easy to be green?

It was Kermit the Frog. Remember?

But me and my friend Zac aren't just a pair of Muppets!

We're old Etonians!

And there's a big difference!

So, lets get down to being cool to stop the world getting warm!

❶ Always cycle to work, even if your chauffeur has to drive behind you with all your important documents, iPods, clean shoes, change of underwear and top hat.

Another great thing about having your chauffeur driving behind you is that if you get tired, you can always throw the bike away and hop into the back!

❷ Always use the bus or the train. That way you get to know what it feels like to be an ordinary person, before your helicopter takes you back to London!

❸ Never wear a tie!

Do you realise that tying a tie uses up 340 kilowatts of energy that could otherwise power a small wind turbine!

Also making ties wastes thousands of acres of valuable tie forest in Thailand!

Simply leave your tie with your chauffeur, and he'll jet it off to you, wherever you are in the world.

❹ Another good tip is to get someone to grow your own vegetables!

We've got this marvellous little man in the village who comes in once a week.

So there you are!

Signed
Cameron the Frog
Chief Muppet
The New Conservative Party

Vote Conservative for a Green Planet!

"My God, Fothergill – they're not King or Emperor –
they're Führer Penguins!"

GLENDA SLAGG

FLEET STREET'S LAP-TOP DANCER!!?

■ HATS and everything else off to Bonny Prince Harry, who's not frightened to go with his army buddies for a naughty night out a-leerin' and a-peerin' at leggy lap-dancers in Heathrow's fashionable Spearmint Rhino!?! What hot-blooded male wouldn't do the same to let off a bit of steam after a hard day's grillin' and a-drillin' on the Sandhurst Parade Ground!?!! God bless you, Sire!!!?! What girl wouldn't be honoured to help you stand to attention!!?! Geddit!!?! I bet you did!!? Geddit?!?

■ PRINCE HARRY?!? What a disgrace!??!! An officer of Her Majesty's Armed Forces reduced to seeing a sordid sex-show in seedy Slough!!!?! What are we supposed to think when the grandson of the Queen of England is seen a-droolin' and a-dribblin' at the antics of some sleazy slapper stickin' her wotsit up against a greased pole??!??!? Get back to barracks, Your Royal Randyness and have a cold shower!!?!

Byeeee!!!

Court Circular

Mustique

His Royal Highness the Prince William will today visit a luxury yacht and unveil a pair of flowery swimming trunks. He will be attended by the Girlfriend Royal, Miss Kate Fruity, wearing a formal turquoise bikini. His Royal Highness will then proceed into the sea where he will be presented with a series of dive bombs by Charlie Ricketson-Smythe, the Old Etonian Poursuivante, and Rupert Rupertson, the Bloody-Good-Bloke-in-Waiting. The Royal Party will then get annoyed by the arrival of the Gentlemen of the Press.

That Procession In Full

1st Jet Ski

Mr Jason Filth of Filthpix

2nd Jet Ski

Mr Len Scap of Blurry Snaps International

1st Lilo

Signor Slizi Paparazzi of Paris Snatch Magazine

1st Inflatable Dolphin

Mr Jonathan Isaby of the London Evening Standard

'I DID NOT SLEEP WITH JOHN PRESCOTT'

Woman's Shock Claim

by Our Political Staff **Lunchtime O'Bonk** (and Teatime as well)

TRISH DULL, a high-flying £12,500-a-year school dinner lady from Cleethorpes, shocked the nation yesterday when she admitted that she had never had an affair with the Deputy Prime Minister.

Said the 64-year-old mother of eight, as she broke down on a Radio Five Live phone-in, "Yes, it's true – Mr Prescott never groped me at a party or asked me for oral sex.

"I know this will shock a lot of people", sobbed Mrs Dull, "But in fact I never even met him."

Full story and pictures pp 2-14

HOW THE CABINET WORKS

Sorry I'm late – something came up

"Selling a kidney was bad enough..."

the Joy of Secretaries

The Gourmet Guide to cringe-making by international Secs Expert Dr Alex Discomfort

The following positions have been recommended for use between consenting Deputy Ministers and their secretaries

THE RED BOX

Gary Andrews

The man sits at the desk reading his briefings on regeneration and the environment.

The woman gets under the table and addresses the Honorable Member.

THE TWO JAGUARS

The man sits in the back of his car refusing to comment before transferring to his other car to avoid the press.

The woman sits in the Mail on Sunday "talking dirty".

THE "UNTENABLE" POSITION

The man kneels in front of the Prime Minister in submission.

Meanwhile, the other man carries on screwing the country.

PRESCOTT SECRETARY SELLS DIARY FOR £250,000

It's money for old grope

NORFOLK BIRD FLU OUTBREAK

30,000 birds get flu...

None of them sleep with John Prescott...

So no one cares...

... Er, that's it.

BLAIR ANNOUNCES NEW DREAM TEAM

by Our Political Staff Peter O'Bore

IN THE most dramatic Cabinet reshuffle since Harold McWilson's notorious "Night of the Long Trousers" in 1978, Prime Minister Tony Blair has kept on the same bunch of dead-beats as before. *(Is this right? Ed.)*

● **Out goes disgraced Deputy Prime Minister, JOHN PRESCOTT.**

● **In comes JOHN PRESCOTT, Deputy Prime Minister in disgrace.**

● **Out goes thuggish bruiser and former Communist, DR JOHN REID.**

● **In comes DR JOHN REID, statesmanlike safe pair of hands.**

● **Out goes MARGARET BECKETT.**

● **In she comes again.**

● **Out goes TONY BLAIR to announce that he is staying on for ever.**

THOSE CABINET CHANGES IN FULL

Minister Without Portfolio **Ruth Kelly**

Minister Without Trousers **John Prescott**

(That's enough appointments. Ed.)

62-YEAR-OLD WOMAN 'TO HAVE JOB'

by Our Medical Staff Dr Patricia Rashbrook

A 62-year-old woman has become the first-ever woman to be made Foreign Secretary.

She said yesterday: "It's a miracle. I am over the hill... I mean the moon.

"All my life I have longed to have a little job and now, thanks to the amazing Tony Blair and his Futility Treatment, my dream has come true."

Blair Babe

But there are many critics who are appalled and claim Mrs Beckett is far too old to cope with the demands of a new job.

Going Into New Labour

"What will she do," asked one outraged observer (Mr J. Straw), "with the sleepless nights, the temper tantrums and the constant crying of Mr Blair?"

He concluded: "Mrs Beckett is at an age when she should be thinking about having a baby, not becoming Foreign Secretary."

"So, Mr Darwin. You say he followed you home from the Galapagos?"

ROMAN TIMES

Kalends of April 44 B.C.　　　　Price Two Denarii (only on Monday)

CAESAR STILL NOT ASSASSINATED SHOCK

BY OUR POLITICAL STAFF PETRUS O'BORUS

THE ROMAN people were disappointed as the Ides of March came and went without the predicted assassination of Antonius Caesar.

Said leading conspirator Gordonius Brutus, "Look, I've made it clear that it's time for renewal and that we must move forward. The people have given the senate a wake up call saying that they're fed up with all the sleaze and pointless invasions of other countries."

But Brutus's words fell far short of the expected knife in the back and the feeling in the Senate is that the Dictator will stay on for as long as he can in order to stop Brutus seizing control.

Said Antonius Caesar, "Et non tu, Gorde?" *(cont. XCIV)*

Advertisement

Have you got election problems?

Dr Gordon Brown writes

❝One in three labour candidates admits suffering from "election loss". This is nothing to be ashamed about and is entirely due to factors beyond your control – i.e. impotence at the very top of the body politic.

I promise that I can restore health and vigour to even the most flaccid member.

Order my booklet at once **The Role of Britain in the New World Order** (*Bloomsbury* £39.99) and you too will once again enjoy being up in the polls.❞

Those Local Election Results In Full

Dollis Hill (South)

Tristram Bicycle-Clip *(Green Conservative Party)* **271**;
Ron Sleaze *(Labour)* **31**;
Simon Lovetrouser *(Liberal Democrat All Night Party)* **57**;
Reg Himmler *(BNP)* **35**;
Daisy Windfarm *(Green Green Party)* **2**; Ayatollah Saddam Galloway *(Respect or Die Party)* **24**;
Tory Gain.

dawes

ARE YOU A SPIDER?

I'M A FRAYED KNOT

59

This Film Could Destroy The Church

Reveals BORIS JOHNSON

CRIPES! Blimey! Apparently, there's this film which proves that Jesus had lots of kids, and that many of his descendants are still alive today. Possibly including you, readers! And even me. Well,

strike a light. As we all know, it was the 4th-Century Gnostic Bishop Borisius, founder of the Gnomic heresy, who first came up with this old chestnut at the Council of Davinci in 425BC. As we Greek speakers put it – Was Jesus *homoeroticus* or *homoldetonius?* But it was not until Hollywood really looked into it that the whole bally cover-up was finally *(continued 94 BC)*

"Out with the lads converting heathens, my eye! I'll wager you were off changing water into wine again... When are you going to change something useful, like a baby's nappy, Mr High-and-Mighty?"

Why Jesus Would Never Have Married And Had Children...

POLLY FILLER

SO it's official! Working mothers are fitter, healthier and slimmer than stay-at-home puddings who spend all their time eating cakes and watching Noel Edmonds!

This comes as no surprise to yours truly, who has been juggling the tightrope of modern motherhood, successful relationships and a high-flying career writing best-sellers, for years! Just dip into *Mummy For Old Tightrope* (Tyrell and Pearson £19.99), *The Curse Of The Yummy Mummy!* (Johnson and Johnson £29.99) or *Nanny Is The Root Of All Evil – A Sideways Look At Hopeless Girls From Somalia!* (Useless Simon and Shuster £39.99) and you'll

see why I've got a figure to die for! (And I don't just mean sales of my latest book – no. 94 on Amazon, thanks for asking!)

NO, we working media mums know full well that the best way to lose weight and look great is to use up thousands of calories shouting at the au-pair for putting toddler Charlie's microwaveable Narnia character chicken nuggets in the dishwasher!! (A hilarious anecdote in all my books, but not so funny for poor Famina who got sent back to the remains of her village with a flea in her ear and a bill for £3.99 for the ruined nuggets!!)

And who needs the gym when you have to run up the stairs every night to tell your useless partner to stop watching Richard Hammond's *World of Exploding Toilets* on Sky Desperate 6 and go and do Charlie's prep! You're obviously too busy yourself, writing an amusing account of how stay-at-home dumplings are even fatter than the cakes they eat all day whilst watching Noel Edmonds!

So the recipe is pretty obvious, isn't it, sisters? As I said to our ditsy new girl, Hunga from Zimbabwe, only this morning, "Work more and eat less!"

© Polly Filler 2006.

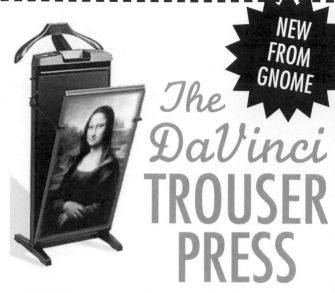

NEW FROM GNOME

The DaVinci TROUSER PRESS

RELIVE all the thrills of the blockbuster film of the book of the millennium with the Trouser Press that Christ's descendants would have used if he had fathered a child and gone to live in Boulogne!

ENJOY the biggest mystery of the last 2000 years whilst steaming your favourite trousers, just as all the Knights Templars have done from Galileo to Michelangelo to Wayne Rooney.

PLUS! Can you solve this mystic code that has been handed down by the secretive Brothers of Corby for generations and which is inscribed on each and every Trouser Press?

"If I had to condemn one trouser press as heretical, I would have no hesitation in condemning the Gnome DaVinci Trouser Press" **His Holiness the Pope.**

A Mad Nine Wait*

Send £666 now to: Gnome Trouser Press Offer The Trading Estate Crawley.

*Made in Taiwan

Hollywood Movies You Won't See

Day 18,250. The housemates are celebrating their half-century in the Big Brother house.

11.15 am. Mikey and Richard have wrapped up well and are in the garden. Glyn is having a bit of a cough. His back's been playing up again. Imogen and Lea are making their way on their zimmer frames to the living area. Satnav and Cornflake, who only joined the house thirty-two years ago, are in the kitchen, getting their bearings. Nikki is in the diary room. She's left her teeth somewhere but she can't remember where.

NIKKI: I'm bored shitless she really does my head in she's gonna push me so far one of these days she so really fucks me off so much I fuckin swear it does my head in.

BB: Today, Nikki, you have been in the Big Brother house for fifty years. You are now seventy three years of age. Nikki – how do you feel?

NIKKI: I'm bored shitless she really does my head in she's gonna push me so far one of these days she so really fucks me off so much I fuckin swear it does my head in.

BB: Thank you, Nikki. You may now leave the diary room.

NIKKI: Big Brother? One more thing.

BB: Yes, Nikki?

NIKKI: I'm bored shitless she really does my head in she's gonna push me so far one of these days she so really fucks me off so much I fuckin swear it does my head in.

BB: Thank you, Nikki.

11.23 am: Nikki and Richard are in the kitchen.

NIKKI: Have you just eaten them? They was my false teeth, they were and now you've gone and fuckin eaten them. You're a fuckin moron. Just go away. I so can't believe you just done that.

11.25 am: Glyn and Camshaft are in the garden. Glyn has had a thought.

GLYN. You know they say every cloud's got silver lino, right? Well, I've like looked and it's so not true.

CAMSHAFT: Lining, babes.

GLYN: Eh?

CAMSHAFT: Not silver lino, babes. Silver lining.

GLYN: Oh. Right. I'll take another look, then.

BIG BROTHER 2056

11.27 am: Aisleyne and Imogen are in the kitchen.

AISLEYNE: How long we been in here then?

IMOGEN: Where?

AISLEYNE: Here?

IMOGEN: Here?

AISLEYNE: Yeah. Here.

IMOGEN: Fifty years, babes.

AISLEYNE: Fifty fuckin' years?

IMOGEN: Yeah.

AISLEYNE: Oh. Right. I gotta do something about these hair extensions.

11.31am: Richard and Laptop are in the garden. Richard is watching paint dry.

RICHARD: This paint's really getting on my fuckin' *TITS* it is. It so takes that long to dry, it's a fuckin' jerk. And the fuckin' wall as well, it's just as fuckin' bad. D'you know what I mean?

LAPTOP: You gotta be strong, Richard. You gotta be strong for all of us. You're gonna get through this, mate, I know you are. Come on, babes. Give us a hug. That's better.

RICHARD (sobs): It's just that the fuckin' paint's been drying BEHIND my back, that's what I can't fuckin' BEAR! It's just so fuckin' TWO-FACED!

LAPTOP: Here's some fuckin' tissue, babes. Take a big fuckin' blow.

11.33 am: Lea comes into the garden.

LEA: What's the matter with him?

LAPTOP: It's so the paint. It's ultra fuckin'' paranoid. It won't fuckin' dry, just because we're lookin' at it. It's just lyin' there drippin', givin' out negative vibes.

LEA: I so like hate that fuckin' paint. It's always slaggin' people off and it just looks through you and make you feel like rubbish, know what I mean.

LAPTOP: C'mon, babes. You gotta be strong. Let's go and watch some grass grow.

LEA: I hate the fuckin' grass, the way it grows so slow, like it thinks it's so fuckin' SUPERIOR. That grass is so fuckin' paranoid, I can't bear it.

11.36am: Nikki and Satnav are in the kitchen

NIKKI: Remember wosisface?

SATNAV: Who?

NIKKI: You know. Wosisfuckinface. Thassit. Frank. What fuckin' happened to Frank, then? He fuckin' voted out, was he?

SATNAV: No fuckin' way. He only fuckin' went and fuckin' DIED, didn't he?

NIKKI: When was that, then?

SATNAV: Eight, nine years ago. Maybe ten. Old fuckin' age.

NIKKI: Oh. Right. Yeah. See if I care. Used to so get on my fuckin' tits, he did. I really liked him and I got a lot of respect for him, but he got on my fuckin' tits he did. So what did we do with the fuckin' corpse, then?

SATNAV: Big Brother made us bury it in the garden. It was startin' to piss me right off anyway, rotting and smelling and that. Least Big Brother gave us a luxury fuckin' hamper in return.

NIKKI: I hate corpses. They're so two-fuckin'-faced.

11. 41 am: Lea is in the diary room. Lea's bosoms are in the garden.

BB: Lea, you have been nominated for eviction by your fellow housemates 3726 times over the past half-century but you are still here. How are you feeling?

LEA: I've been bored fuckin' shitless these past 50 fuckin' years.

BB: Lea, during your time in the Big Brother house, you've performed your own breast enlargement 17 times. They are now a housemate in their own right, and come into the diary room by themselves. Unfortunately, Lea, they can't stop slagging you off behind your back. Why do you think that is?

LEA: I'm just too fuckin' real for them.

As told to
C R A I G   B R O W N

CHANNEL FOUR IN TOURETTE'S SHOCK

by Our Media Staff **Phil Space**

A HUGE storm erupted yesterday over the appearance of Channel Four on national television.

"Night after night we are witnessing a continual stream of obscenities, filth and four-letter words from this disturbed young channel," said one shocked mental health expert. "The channel is clearly suffering from an advanced case of Tourette's Syndrome.

Borette's Syndrome

"It clearly cannot help itself. Every programme it shows has to be about violence, pornography or sexual perversions, punctuated by involuntary outbursts of the 'F' word every other minute."

A leading psychiatrist said, "It is sad and demeaning for Channel Four to be put on television, just so that millions of viewers can laugh at its mental deficiencies."

Channel Fourette's

But TV bosses hit back, saying that the decision to put Channel Four on air was "a brave one, as it shows the public just how bad television programmes are".

"Bedlam is not cruel at all, it's an interesting reality-based social experiment"

Sad at news

IT'S ALL OVER!

Love Split Shocks World
A Nation Mourns

By Our Showbiz Staff John, Paul, George and Ring O'Booze

THE greatest romance of modern times is finished

That was the shock news from Downing Street yesterday when a tearful spokesman confirmed that, after nine years, two weeks and three days, Gordon and Tony have agreed to part.

Said a close friend of the couple, "This is a tragedy, but they just can't live under the same roof any more.

Satanic Mills

"The rows have got worse and worse. The problem is that Gordon became jealous of Tony's fame and good looks.

"Gordon wanted to be a star in his own right – not just to be known as Tony's other half."

Unlucky Heather

In recent months, friends have noticed that the couple have spent more time apart, with Gordon constantly flying off to Africa to promote his charity causes.

Another close friend admitted, "Tony has obviously been under a lot of stress, even bursting into tears on occasion."

"The trouble is," said yet another close friend, "is that Tony can't handle getting older and not being the wonder kid at No. 1 as he was all those years ago."

Mug of Kintyre

"It's all a far cry," said one more of these close friends that we keep inventing, "from that first magical moment when their eyes met over a restaurant table in a trendy Islington restaurant.

"Tony promised Gordon the earth," continued this friend. "The pair became inseparable, and it looked as though their love would last forever."

"But now," chipped several more of these hundreds of close friends "the dream has shattered and Gordon is demanding £800 billion from taxpayers as his share of the settlement."

How They Aren't Related Any More

Paul McCartney   His Money

"You're right, we have stopped"

GLENDA SLAGG
FLEET STREET'S NUMBER ONE HIT GIRL!!!?!

■ SHED A tear for poor, sad Macca as his world crumbles apart!?! Here's a young mop-haired Scouser who's kept our feet a-dancin' and a-prancin' with his magical matchless melodies from yesteryear. But when it came to love, Cupid's arrow missed the Merseyside maestro by a mile!?!? Our hearts go out as one to the lovelorn lyricist from Liverpool, who gave us such unforgettable hits as *(subs – fill in names of unforgettable hits please!)*. We love you, Macca – even if she doesn't!?!?!?!

■ PAUL McCARTNEY!?!?!? You'd have to have a heart of stone not to larf!?!? The only one who couldn't see what was coming to him was the randy old goat himself!?!! There's no fool like an old fool, they say?!??!! And now you've proved them right with a capital 'R'!!?! Tell you what, Macca. You might be sad. But we're not – we're laughing our heads off!!?!!

■ SHED A tear for poor, sad Heather Mills, the feisty lass who came from nowhere to become Britain's First Lady of Pop!?!! Selfless and warm-hearted, she gave him everything – and rescued him from a lonely old age, just when he needed it most!!?! And now the dream has ended. All you needed was love, love, love!!?! And all you got in return was hate, hate, hate!!?! You'd need a heart of stone not to weep for Macca's Mournful Madonna today!!?!!

■ HEATHER MILLS!?!?!? Aren'tcha-sickofher???!? So Macca's finally woken up to the fact that her real name is "Little Miss Gold-Digger 2006"!!?! Come off it, Heather!!? The only thing that attracted you was the size of his bank balance!!!?! You saw a vacancy for "Lady Macca" and you got the job!?! More like "Lady Muck", if you ask me!!?! You may have fooled Macca, but you haven't fooled Auntie Glenda!!?! So take your money and hop it!?!?! (Geddit?!!?)

■ *LINDA McCARTNEY!!? Don'tcha-missher?!? I know at the time I said she was a loopy vegetarian who couldn't sing and looked like the back end of a bus!!!?! But compared to the present Mrs Macca, lovely Linda shines out like a candle in the wind?!! All together now – "Lady McCartney, children at your feet..."*

■ HERE THEY are – Glenda's Maypole Munchies!

● **Thierry Henry!!?!** OK, so he' didn't score in Paris but he can have a second chance round at my place!!?!

● **Tom Hanks?!??** OK, so you're stiff and boring!!?! I don't mind as long as you forget the boring bit!!?? Geddit??!!

● **Mahmoud Ahmedinajad!!?!** Crazy name, completely crazy guy!!?!

Byeeee!!!

I've been sold a pup

Aww... look at him, with his big sad eyes, all helpless and waiting to be skinned

Ross Kemp is Great! It's official! p94

LOVESICK OLD FOOL CONNED BY RUTHLESS GOLDDIGGER

by Rebekah Filth

A RICH elderly billionaire has been taken to the cleaners by a scheming fortune hunter who is young enough to be his daughter.

Yes, poor 93-year-old Rupert Murdoch, known as "Mucker" because of the filth he prints in his newspapers, fell hopelessly in love with Wendy Dung, the ambitious, scheming two-legged temptress from the land of Egg Fried Rice.

When I'm 94

Within minutes of the wedding bells ringing out, the Dirty Gold Digger was up the duff and making a claim on Mucker's media millions.

■ THE SUN SAYS

How stupid can you get, Mucker?

She even made you do strenuous oriental yoga to try and kill you off and get her hands on your *(cont p.94)*

CHRISTIAN AID WEEK

Give – And Give Generously!!!

Tony, Dave and Ming are all the victims of a terrible shortage of money which has recently hit Britain's politicians.

Their traditional sources of income have dried up, virtually overnight, thanks to a change in the climate, not to mention investigations by police.

There is only one way that these three unhappy men (one of them an elderly Chinaman) can hope to survive this cruel downturn in their fortunes.

That is if you, the great British public, rally around and dig deep to provide the funds they so desperately need.

- £10,000 will buy a nice new tie and haircut
- £250,000 will buy a new specially-equipped 'battle bus'
- £1,000,000 will buy a peak-time TV election broadcast, produced by Bargleby, Bowtie and Glasses.
- £2 million will buy you a peerage (*shurely shome mishtake? WD*)

Just send donations at once to the Party Funding Account, the Inland Revenue. Failure to pay on time could result in imprisonment or death.

By order J. STRAW
Leader of the House of Commons and Minister for Lords Reform and State Funding for Political Parties.

WATER COMPANIES' NEW WARNING

*by Our Drought Staff **Stan Pipe***

WATER companies were warning customers last night that the reservoirs of money were "not as full as they would like".

Said a spokesman, "Normally we have lakes full of cash, buckets full of the stuff sloshing around everywhere, but this year we've taken so much out in dividends that our stocks are severely depleted."

Customers are being urged to save money and not waste it needlessly on non-essentials.

Hosepipe Bank

"Use as little money as possible this summer," reads a new nationwide campaign, "because you'll need it to pay your enormous water bill later in the year."

"It could be time for a hosepipe ban, Arthur"

Advertisement

NEW FROM GNOMA

The Incredible Football Boot That Will Change Your Life

The Metatarsal™

● Following years of research, footwear technologists at the Gnoma Laboratories in Somalia have developed a revolution in advanced soccological innovation. Made from new, super-lightweight, recycled cardboard, the **Metatarsal** looks just like a normal boot, but as soon as you put it on, your foot immediately breaks in several places and you're out for the rest of the season!! Works every time!!

Says international star W.R., *"Aaargh!!"*

Send now for your pair of Metatarsals and be on crutches in minutes!

Price: £79.99 (laces extra)

Colours: Manchester Red, Chelsea Blue, Newcastle Brown

SIX TO WATCH IN THE WORLD CUP

COURT CIRCULAR

🏐 **Noleen McCleavage**, 19. Gorgeous, pouting ex-tracksuit model. Noleen is looking forward to eating hamburgers in Hamburg with her fiancé, Shane Wayney (Liverpool United).

🏐 **Shelley Blondie**, 22. Gorgeous, pouting one-time Miss Chorleywood (2001). Shelley is a high-flying dental assistant who is looking forward to shopping in Munich's fashionable HitlerPlatz shopping precinct. Girlfriend of Rio Tinto-Zinc (Bolton Albion).

🏐 **Michelle Totty**, 28. Fiery, gorgeous, pouting former RyanAir flight attendant who is looking forward to sampling the bier kellers of downtown Dusseldorf. Ex-wife of Sebastian Wright-Wheatcroft (Tottenham Wanderers) and current girlfriend of his cousin Damien Dancona (Chelsea City).

🏐 **Karen Bikini**, 23. Thai-born, gorgeous, pouting masseuse who is looking forward to networking with the tired football managers of Stuttgart. Partner of Jermaine Greer (West Bromwich Wednesday) and mother of some of his children.

🏐 **Debbie Shagwell**, 17. Chigwell-born, gorgeous, pouting, phew! What a scorcher! Blimey! *(That's enough Six To Watch. Ed.)*

Beckingham Palace, Saturday

His Royal Highness the Earl of Beckham and Lady Poshina Beckswell were delighted to hold a reception in honour of the National Association Football Team. They received the following distinguished guests.

1st Limo
Sir Spudface Nipper and Lady De Rooney

2nd Limo
Sir Oswald Osbore, Lady Sharonita Osbore and the Hon Kelly Osbore.

1st Stretch Limo
Sir Gordon Ramsay of Fuckington; Lady Cocaina Moss of that Priory; Dame Elton and Lady John; Baroness Hurley of the Front page of the Daily Telegraph; Sir Robbington Williams; Sir Fredswell Flinstone and Lady Flinstone.

1st Minicab
The Duchess Fergiana of Weight-Watchers and her daughter Princess Fergianella

1st Pram
Master Theo Walcott

1st Gatecrasher (on bicycle)
David "Dave" Cameron, the guest of Dame Rebekkah Filth.

(That's enough distinguished guests. Ed)

EXCLUSIVE TO ALL NEWSPAPERS EVERY DAY

THAT ALL-PURPOSE WORLD CUP PIECE IN FULL

by Phil Boots

Yes! Wayne Rooney is definitely on the way to Germany / never going to make it.

Doctors were agreed last night that Wayne's foot was healing fast/worse than ever.

The Rooney metatarsal saga is over at last/set to continue and England can now expect to bring the Cup home/crash out in the early stages.

Make no mistake. This is the best/worst news we've had since I wrote this piece yesterday.

Watch out/don't worry Germany! The World Cup is coming home/we're coming home.

Subbuteo Footballers' Wives

ON OTHER PAGES

Iraq meltdown 92
Afghanistan meltdown 93
Earthquake in Java 94

"Can I borrow a cup of water?"

BANX

NEW FROM GNOME

The World Cup TROUSER PRESS

ALL the thrills of the greatest football tournament in the world are yours with the Gnome World Cup Trouser Press!

As the world's finest footballers battle it out on the playing fields of Frankfurt, you can press your trousers in the comfort of your own home!

Approved by UEFA, FIFA and DEFRA, this wonderful themed clothing accessory will, in years to come, become a priceless heirloom for you, your children and your children's trousers.

FLY THE FLAG WHILST PRESSING YOUR TROUSERS AND BELIEVE THE DREAM!

Says famous England Coach, **Sven Goran Eriksson**, "Whenever I meet my lady friends and take off my trousers, I make sure they are in tip top condition when I put them on again."

Send £1966 now to: **Gnome Patriotic Trouser Press Offer, Unit 5, Shanghai Trading Estate, Republic of China.**

*Flag designed by world-famous flagologist Sir Geraldino Scarfini, FRGS, NBG.

WETTEST DROUGHT SINCE RECORDS BEGAN

MILLIONS of home-owners were drowning yesterday in the torrential droughts that are threatening to wash away the whole of the South-East of the Country.

(Reuters)

KEITH RICHARDS BRAIN OPERATION

He's mumbling, he can't remember anything and he's staggering about looking terrible

It's an amazing recovery

GNOMEBY'S

BOND STREET & ABU DHABI

Sale of Highly Important Objets D'Art and Memorabilia, formerly the property of Her Late Royal Highness the Princess Margaret, Countess of Rothman.

Lot 1
Very Significant Porcelain Ashtray, inscribed 'A Souvenir of Mustique', showing hand-painted scene of natives and palm trees, c. 1966. Artist anonymous. On reverse the legend 'Made in China'.
Estimated price £12,500.00.

Lot 2
16cm Cigarette Holder in Ebony-style plastic, ornamented with diamond-style glazing, believed to be a personal gift from the late Peter Sellers.
Estimated price £800,000.00.

Lot 3
Clipper Cigarette Lighter, fashioned in translucent plastic and bearing the inscription 'Put a Tiger in your Tank', believed to be a gift from the Hon. Colin Tennant.
Estimated price £1000.00.

Lot 4
Pair Garden Secateurs, in mint condition. Still in box, with card attached 'Happy Christmas Your Highness, see you Thursday at my place, love Roddy" (the Honourable Roderick Llewellyn, second son of the Lord Llewellyn of Horsebox).
Estimated price £250,000.00.

Lot 5
Set of 3,000 Gin Bottles, empty. A collection dating from various periods, curated by the Earl of Snowdon and others, including the following brands: Gilbey's, Gordon's, Plymouth, Bombay, Hiroshima, Tesco Own Brand.
Estimated price £0.25.

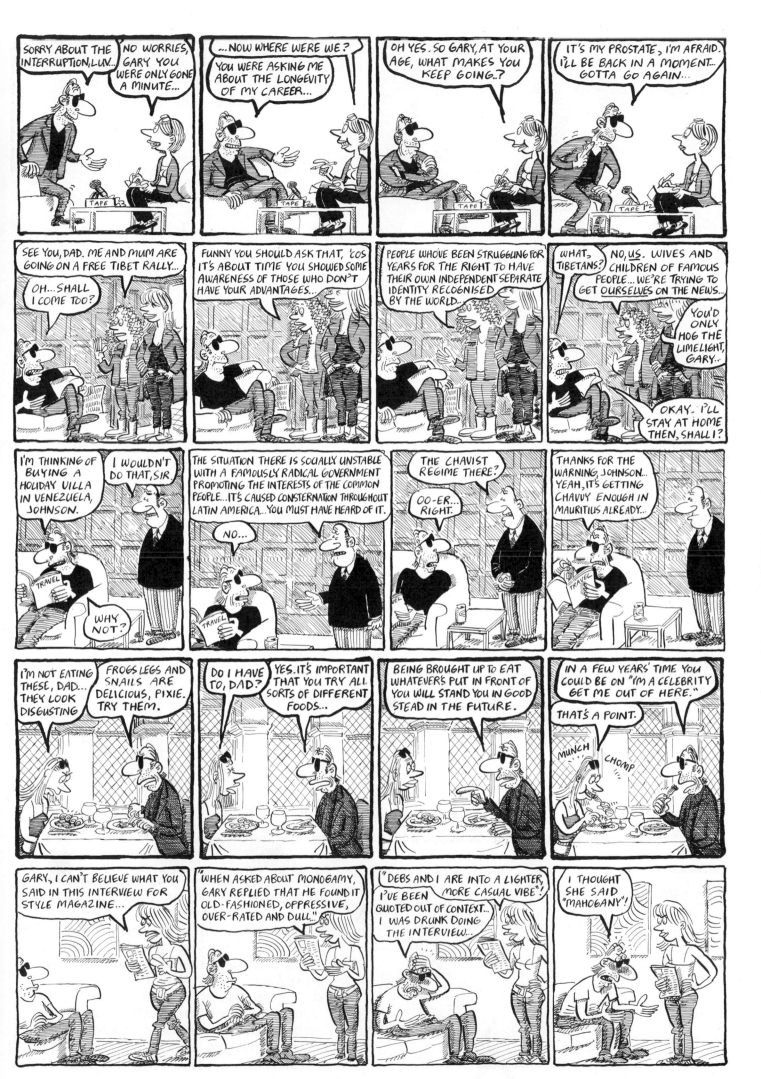

DIANA
— STILL DEAD
Knacker's Amazing Claim

by Our Man At The Wye-on-Wye Festival
Alan Rubbisher

IN A SHOCK, off-the-cuff disclosure at the prestigious Wye-on-Wye Literary Festival, Britain's No. 1 policeman, Lord Inspector "Knacker of the Yard" Knacker, revealed that he had written a book called *Even Stevens: My Life In Crime.*

The cream of Britain's literary glitterati sat open-mouthed as Lord Knacker let slip that his new book was now on sale at all bookshops (Waterstone's) and that its price would be a very reasonable £24.99 (although a three-for-two discount was currently being offered by Tesco).

After he had spoken for 40 minutes about the availability of his volume, Lord Knacker took questions, the first of which was "Is it not true that your investigation into the death of Princess Diana has been a complete waste of time and money?"

Not Much Cop

"On the contrary," replied Britain's leading detective, "we have unearthed astonishing new evidence which shows conclusively that Princess Diana is dead, and that the Establishment version of events, ie that she was abducted by aliens whilst pregnant by a direct descendant of the Pharaoh King Fayed the Third, can now be discounted."

Lord Knacker's book can be obtained directly from the Eye Bookline at a discounted price of £39.99.

HOME OFFICE WORKER HAD NO RIGHT TO BE THERE

By Our Political Staff **Peter O'Bore**

A 65-YEAR-OLD Scotsman with a communist record was found working in the Home Office last week. Mr Reid had no papers and no qualifications but claimed he had been given the job "because there was no one else".

Mr Reid has had a number of jobs in the last five years since he entered the country from his native Scotland. He once had a temporary job working in hospitals and even had a sensitive post in a defence related office.

As soon as the mistake was discovered, nothing was done. Mr Reid was allowed to continue to come in and work provided he made no attempt to "tidy up the mess".

Said a spokesperson, "We have no idea how many Scotsmen there are in Westminster but estimates suggest anything between two or three thousand or maybe fifteen or maybe none at all. We have no idea about anything" said the spokesman.

THAT TORY A-LIST

by Our Political Staff **Peter O'Bore**

WHO ARE they, the exciting new A-list celebrities who have become a must-have fashion accessory for every go-ahead local Tory association that wants to lose the next election?

1. **Lulu Lipstick**, 25. High-flying lesbian hedge fund manager of City firm Goldfinger Asset Management. Says Lulu, "My Number One political pin-up is David Blair, or is it Tony Cameron? I'm a bit new to this political game."

2. **Goldman Zac**, 21. High-flying son of the late billionaire Sir Jams Goldfinger. Says Zac, "I'm not interested in politics, but David really passionately believes in saving the planet and that kind of thing, and anyway we were at school together."

3. **Ranjit Dipstick**, 27. High-flying soap star who played the first gay Asian turkey farmer in *Emmerdale*. His passionate embrace with the new gay vet was a landmark moment in British television. Says Ranjit, "This is the Lib Dems I'm joining, isn't it?"

4. **General Wellbeing**, 108. High-flying First World War veteran and a fellow member of White's with David Cameron's great-grandfather. Got on the list entirely by mistake. Says Sir Horace, "Don't quote me, old boy, but this Cameron chap is a bit of a twit, if you ask me." *(That's enough A-list celebs. Ed.)*

Late News

General Wellbeing chosen for first available seat by local Tories **94**

Advertisement

YES IT'S THE NEW BOND!

The legendary British spy is back in an explosive new adventure – DR NO SURRENDER (surely some mistake?). The name's McGuinness... Martin McGuinness! Join him as he takes on the paranoid Dr Paisley and his sidekick with the Bowler Hat! (Are you sure this is right? Ed.) Thrill to the man who likes a molotov cocktail, shaken not stirred (that's enough Bond, Ed.).

IRAQ: HADITHA SHOCK

There wasn't a massacre and there wasn't a cover-up

Tell it to the Marines!

CORRUPTION BARS ENTRY TO EU

by Our Brussels Staff **Hans Intill**

THE EU last night slammed the door on its latest two would-be members, Bulgaria and Romania, on the grounds that they failed to meet the EU's "corruption criteria".

Said an EU spokesman, Piotr Mandelssohn, "We have very strict rules about this kind of thing, and I'm afraid our Bulgarian and Romanian friends have fallen seriously short.

"We accept," he said, "that they are both very corrupt, but until they can match the degree of corruption shown by Chirac's France, Berlusconi's Italy and Blair's Britain, there can be no hope of them being given entry."

LATE NEWS

Nigeria and Somalia to join EU.

BLAIR ATTACKS HIMSELF

by Our Political Staff **Peter O'Bore**

A FURIOUS Prime Minister hit out today at the human rights legislation, which he described as "political correctness gone mad" and "a threat to the British way of life".

He continued: "Whoever brought in this badly-thought-out, shoddy and dangerous piece of legislation should be sacked."

When it was pointed out that it was he himself who had brought in the Act, he said: "You can't sack me. It's a breach of my human rights."

CHINESE PRESIDENT MEETS BILL GATES

Any tips on ruthlessly suppressing all opposition to you?

Funny, I was about to ask you the same question

"Of course I don't need a fork."

—PILBROW—

THE INDEPENDENT

 NEWSPAPER OF THE YEAR

This is meant to be a yet the front  is full of simplistic that treats its readers like . We ask, is taking the ? Or is the going down the ?

AMAZING NEW PICTURE OF PRESCOTT ROCKS GOVERNMENT

by Our Political Staff **Terry Photo-Lenz**

THIS IS the sensational photograph of John Prescott that has sent shock waves around the country.

It clearly shows John Prescott sitting at his desk doing some work. Nowhere in the picture can we see a secretary with her legs around Prescott's neck nor is he hitting any members of the public nor is there any sign of a croquet mallet.

Hard Labour

Said one shocked Labour backbencher, "This is completely unacceptable behaviour. The thought of Prescott actually being in charge of anything will outrage ordinary people throughout the country."

He continued, "Nobody wants to see Prescott actually doing anything important. Why can't he stick to what he's good at, ie being a national laughing stock who makes Blair look almost competent?"

Working Party

However, the Prime Minister immediately defended his deputy, saying, "This is just John being John. What he does in his own office is his own private affair." He concluded, "John Prescott has my complete confidence. Though, to be on the safe side, I have asked him to give up his desk."

CROQUET
HOW IT WORKS

You put your balls down here, and I'll hit them with this mallet

Funny – that's what the wife said

Who Are They, The Frontrunners In The Race To Be Labour's No. 2?

THESE are the six top hopefuls for the job of playing croquet at Dorneywood and having it off with their secretaries (surely *"Deputy Prime Minister"? Ed.*).

1. **Alan Johnson**, high-flying Minister in the Department of Paperclips. Formerly aide to Geoff Hoon and strongly tipped as the man you haven't heard of. Odds 2/1

2. **John Alanson**, low-flying highflyer from the Ministry of Ministries. Formerly aide to Peter Hoon and known as a pro-Blair Brownite. Odds 7/2

3. **Mrs Harriet Blears**, highflying former Deputy Director for Women's Affairs at the Equality Ministry. Staunch ally of pro-Brown Blairite, Margaret Hoon. Odds 8/1

4. **Mrs Bleary Harriet**, highflying mid-ranking Hoonite and former Assistant Minister for Inter-Departmental Communication under Under-Minister Johnson Alanson. Odds 100/30

5. **Ed Millipede**, highflying, low-crawling garden insect who many tip as a natural successor to the Blearite Harriet Hoonman. Odds 50/1

6. **John Prescott**, croquet-loving, sex fiend whose amorous escapades delighted the public in the long, hot summer of (*That's enough frontrunners. Ed.*)

Now You Too Can Be Part Of Dave Cameron's Exciting New Tory Party Of Tomorrow!

A HELP us to choose a new go-ahead logo for the 21st Century, instead of the boring, out-of-date torch that belongs to the bad old days of Mrs Thatcher.

■ **WHAT would you like to see as the iconic symbol of the modern, exciting, go-ahead Cameron Party?**

| Windmill – Green! | Open-Neck Shirt – Casual! | iPod – Modern! | Jelly – Flexible! | Labour Rose – Perfect! |

B NOW you have chosen the logo, would you like to be the next Mayor of London?

You don't have to know much about politics or London, but just complete this simple questionnaire:

1. The current Mayor of London is

a) Ken Livingstone?

b) Wayne Rooney?

c) Sir Peregrine Worsthorne?

2. The Great Fire of London was in

a) Paris?

b) London?

c) Peterborough?

3. The River Thames is

a) a statue?

b) a river?

c) a grapefruit segment?

And now complete the following sentence in not more than 10 words:

"I would like to be Conservative Mayor of London because...........
....
....
....
....
....*"*

C ONGRATULATIONS! You are now Mayor of London and a member of the Conservative Party.

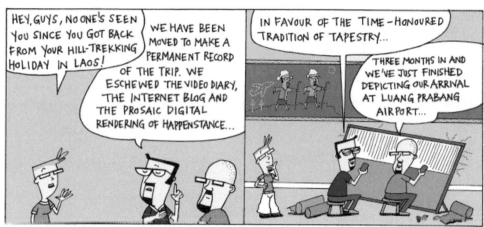

POETRY CORNER

In Memoriam Sir Freddie Laker, The Father Of Low-Cost Air Travel

So. Farewell
Then Sir
Freddie Laker –
The Father of
Low-Cost Air
Travel.

Now you have
Gone to Heaven
On a One-
Way Bargain
Ticket.

Yes, I can
Hear the announcement:
"Will Sir Freddie
Laker go to
Pearly Gate
Number 94 at
Once?"

And are
You I wonder
Now on a
No-Frills
Cloud

Where you have
To bring your
Own harp?

         E.J. Thribb (17½)

**In Memoriam
The Routemaster bus**

So. Farewell then
The Routemaster bus.

For 51 years
The supreme symbol of
London throughout
The world –
But now sadly axed
In favour of the so-called
Bendy bus.

"Hold tight please."
"Room for two more on top."
"Next stop Chelsea
Town Hall."

Yes, those were
Your catchphrases.

Farewell, farewell, farewell.
"Any more farewells
Please?"

     E.J. Thribb (Number 17½)

E.J. Thribb will be signing his latest anthology of poems *A Garland for Global Warming* at the Poetry Bookshop, Wisbech at 9.30am on Christmas Day.

FORESTGATE-GATE – WORLD EXCLUSIVE!!!

PRIVATE EYE has obtained a copy of the top secret intelligence report that led the Metropolitan Police to launch the most daring night-time raid in the history of crime.

It was this astonishing top-secret background briefing note that led Sir Ian Blair and his colleagues to believe that they had no alternative but to cock it up.

"Better to be sorry than safe," said Sir Ian, "although, of course, we are in no way sorry, because we haven't done anything wrong."

THAT MI5 INTELLIGENCE DOSSIER IN FULL

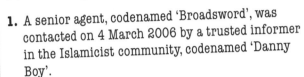

To: M

From: C

For Your Eyes Only

1. A senior agent, codenamed 'Broadsword', was contacted on 4 March 2006 by a trusted informer in the Islamicist community, codenamed 'Danny Boy'.

2. 'Danny Boy' communicated to 'Broadsword' the essentials of a conversation he had overheard on a No. 94 bus running between Ilford Broadway and Forest Gate, East London.

3. The conversation between the two parties in question ran as follows:

   Passenger A: You know those two brothers who live at No. 47?

   Passenger B: No.

   Passenger A: You know, the ones with the bald heads and the funny beards?

   Passenger B: Oh, yeah.

   Passenger A: They're weird, aren't they? Those beards, they somehow don't look right, do they? Do you think they're stuck on?

4. When this information was processed by senior analysts of the Anti-Terrorism Unit, the following conclusion was drawn:

5. Two highly dangerous Muslim terrorists were disguising themselves with false beards, whilst operating an Al Qaeda-style cell in Leytonstone, probably producing chemical weapons in the form of explosive underwear capable of wiping out the population of London five times over within 45 minutes.

6. It was further thought possible that the two men might well be in the course of constructing a full-scale nuclear bomb, with plutonium acquired from eBay.

7. Computer modelling of the two men suggested that the two men could well be a Mr Osama bin Laden and the late Ayatollah Khomeini.

8. In the light of the above evidence, we recommend that an immediate full-scale emergency operation should be mounted to surround the address in question with 5,000 armed men, properly protected with chemical and biological warfare suits, in order to apprehend these highly dangerous terrorist masterminds – ie, the men with beards.

9. For security reasons, we recommend that the community should not be alerted to the danger by evacuating them to a safe distance from the site of the likely nuclear/chemical explosion, ie 200 kilometres.

10. For operational reasons, agent 'Danny Boy' has gone into hiding and cannot be contacted to confirm any of his evidence, but 'Broadsword' says that he is "not a bad chap for a towelhead".

"You're not the doctor I had last time!"

Hands up who hates the Tories!

BLAIR DEFENDS INVASION OF FOREST GATE

by Our Terrorism Staff **W.M. Deedes**

THE PRIME Minister today defended the invasion of a house in Lansdown Road, Forest Gate, insisting that "Weapons of Mass Destruction" would eventually be found there.

The invasion, by 250 crack police marksmen and chemical warfare experts, was based, he said, on "foolproof evidence contained in a dossier compiled by the intelligence services".

"It may take time," he continued, "to find the weapons in the house, but make no mistake they will be found – unless they have been moved out to a neighbouring borough. Anyway, this is a big house, a one-up, one-down, and there is even a garden shed at the back.

"These weapons could be anywhere or nowhere. As I speak, officers are in a wardrobe upstairs with a torch. Sooner or later they are bound to find something, unless they don't."

Chemical Wardrobe

The Prime Minister was then asked about the unfortunate shooting of various members of the household during the invasion, to which he replied, "It is unfortunate that there have been civilian casualties, but in the war on terror there is bound to be collateral damage."

The Prime Minister finally handed out copies of the intelligence dossier which he had printed out from the internet, which made the sensational claim that deadly mothballs the size of a marble were capable of killing millions of people in Britain **WITHIN 45 MINUTES.**

Weapons of Moth Destruction

"We had no choice," he insisted. "We had to invade and we will stay in Forest Gate for as long as it takes to restore democracy to this troubled borough of East London."

The Deadly Possible Range Of The Unfound Bomb

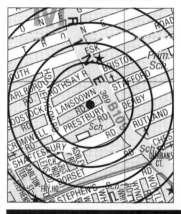

On Other Pages "Bring Our Policemen Home," says Max Hastings **94**

"Nice day for it"

IS THIS EVIL MAN LIVING NEAR YOU?

UNDER new Home Office guidelines, worried parents will be entitled to know if Dr John Reid is at large in their vicinity.

Under the so-called "John's Law", parents can apply to the Home Office to find out the exact whereabouts of the man known as "Reido".

Reido has had a string of aliases (Secretary of State for Education, Defence, Health etc) and has kept constantly on the move in the last few years, making him difficult to track.

Reido has a psychological compulsion to interfere with the law and has recently attacked a number of innocent judges.

Said Mr Justice Cocklecarrot, "No judge is safe whilst this man is at large. The public has a right to know if Reido is lurking round the corner, ready to jump out and make new laws."

Is Reido living in your street? Let us know by contacting our website at once – www.reidophile.con.

Mary Ann Bighead

Hoorah For Father's Day!

Father's Day in the Bighead household was, as ever, a major event. Lots of other families don't bother much about Father's Day, but then they don't have a brilliant hands-on Dad like Mr Bighead who excels at everything, from nappy-changing to discovering the human genome!! And well done me for being so clever as to choose *him* to be father of Intelligencia (8) and Brainella (3) in the first place!

So, whilst other less able families had to make do with a shop-bought card and a pair of socks, in the Bighead family Dad woke up to the sound of the two girls expertly playing a superb cello duet, composed by Brainella. He then opened his special present – a leatherbound volume of Intelligencia's translation of Sir Thomas Aquinas's "Summa Catholicae Fidei Contra Gentiles." from the Latin into rhyming Sanskrit couplets!

Then he had a pot of his favourite Earl Greymatter tea (a Bighead culinary speciality!) and, finally, we all watched a video of me on Question Time being incredible clever. What a perfect day. Poor old other families whose lives aren't as marvellous as mine. Still, it serves them right for not being as clever as me!

© *Mary Ann Bighead 2006.*

Prince Boring

...so, instead of riding into the enchanted forest, I turned right at the magic castle, and.......

The Daily Tottygraph

Fruity Girls Go Shopping!

IN AN amazing development yesterday, some fruity girls went to the shops and bought some things *(Reuters)*

POLLY FILLER

WORLD Cup fever has hit the Filler household! And it's not just the Useless Simon who has gone footie potty, sitting in front of Sky More Plus Extra's Soccer Chat Special with Paul Ross and Kelvin McKenzie!! Yours truly has gone ball barmy as well! Whilst Simon fancies Argentina, I fancy Italy's gorgeous striker, Totti, not to mention Becks, Henry, and anybody in tight shorts called Ronaldo! And I'm not the only one, am I girls?

But there is a downside to both sexes going beautiful-game-bonkers! The washing doesn't get done, the tumble-dryer lies idle, and Simon's underpants remain resolutely unironed! It's domestic meltdown! And why? Because I've had to sack the girl from Angola who wanted to watch the Portugal match instead of cleaning out the oven; then I had to send the girl from Ghana back home because she wanted to watch the Italy game instead of cleaning out the hamster cage; and to cap it all, I had to give the girl from Tobago her marching orders when she asked if she could watch her lot take on Sweden when the toilets needed cleaning!!

HONESTLY, FIFA, if you're going to encourage us women to watch football then you'll have to stop all these developing nations getting into the World Cup! Or the whole world is going to grind to a halt!

Believe me, I've got so desperate that I've had to recruit an au pair from a country with no interest in the World Cup – Scotland! Unfortunately, she keeps demanding to be paid!! Roll on next month when I can send the hopeless and greedy Flora back to McNowheresville and get a nice girl from one of the poorer villages in Paraguay!! Come on, you football!!!

Polly Filler's hilarious World Cup diary *Three Irons on My Shirt – Confessions of a Big Match Mummy!* (£17.99 Johnson and Pearson) is available at all good bookshops.

Those World Cup Acronyms In Full

WAGS	Wives And Girlfriends
SHAGS	Unofficial girlfriends whose numbers appear on footballers' mobile phones
GAGS	Writs served by footballers accused of relationships with SHAGS
HAGS	Unofficial elderly girlfriends of Wayne Rooney
WAG(E)S	Ridiculous sum of footballers' money spent by WAGS, SHAGS, etc.

"Here come the Iranian footballers' wives"

That Degree Citation In Full

SALUTAMUS MICHAELUM DOUGLASI, FAMOSUM STELLUM HOLLYWOODENSIS ET FILIUS KIRKI DOUG-LASI, FAMOSISSIMUM STELLUM HOLLYWOODENSIS IN CINEMATICO CLASSICO NOMINE 'SPARTACUS' ('EGO SUM SPARTACUS. *NON.* EGO SUM SPARTACUS' ETC. ETC.) ATQUE MARITUS AD ZETAM CATHERINAM JONUS, PULCHERRIMAM PUELLAM GALLICORUM FAMOSISSIMAM PER... ER... ER... HONORARUM TE, MICHAELE, PER ACTUM THESPIANORUM MAGNIFICO IN PARTICULARE 'ATTRACTIONE FATALI' ET 'INSTINCTO FUNDAMENTALI' CUM SHARONA LAPIDA (ADULTUS SOLUS XXXX). 'EHU QUOD SCORCHERUS' DICIT TELEGRAPHICUS DIURNALIS *(SATIS EDITORIUM)*.

© UNIVERSITY OF ST ANDREWS MMVI

POLICE LOG

Neasden Central Police Station

1500 hrs Station opens (new office hours)

1501 hrs 999 call received from member of public to report incident of alleged multiple homicide in the Bobby Moore retail complex by Kurdish people-trafficking gang. Unfortunately no officers were available to respond to this call as the entire station staff was engaged in a 90-minute "monitoring exercise" with regard to the Belarus v. Rumbabwe Group D play-off. Officers had been instructed to examine all crowd shots to identify known English football hooligans who might be attending the wrong game.

1700 hrs Armed response unit despatched to Flat B, 135 Crack Crescent, to effect immediate arrest of dangerous council tax evader Mrs Ethel Prunehat, 84. The criminal had refused to pay council tax lawfully due to Neasden Borough Council, on the grounds that, as she alleged, the local police service had failed to take action to prevent her garden shed being turned into the headquarters of the local crack-dealing organisation, and also a 24-hour brothel. This constituted a prima facie libel against the police service, and officers attempted to persuade Mrs Prunehat to withdraw her disgraceful slur before she unfortunately stood in the way of PC Morden's H&K 45mm sub-machine gun when it was accidentally discharged owing to the heavy-duty anti-terrorist rubber gloves which had been issued to PC Morden for health and safety purposes. Mrs Prunehat will not be available to stand trial owing to her decease.

1800 hrs A case conference was held, involving all the officers who had been engaged in examining photographic evidence relating to the recent incident in which several hundred members of the Islamic community had exercised their human right to mount an arson attack on the local Ikea store in the mistaken belief that this Swedish-owned business was in some way connected to inflammatory Danish cartoons showing the Prophet Mohammed assembling a flat-pack shelf unit. After more than 100 hours of intense scrutiny of a close-up photograph showing a Mr Siddiqui al-Bastardi carrying in one hand a placard bearing the words 'Burn All Infidels Now And Cut Off Their Heads' and in the other a box of matches, it was concluded that this did not constitute sufficient evidence to identify Mr Siddiqui. As one officer remarked, "They all look the same." He immediately arrested himself for making a deliberately racist comment likely to cause a breach of the peace, and was suspended on full pay pending an official inquiry.

1900 hrs Report received from MI5 that a middle-aged Caucasian male had been observed in the Whitehall area, carrying a copy of an inflammatory and seditious publication, the Daily Telegraph, with its headline 'Is It Time For Blair To Go?'. This had been rightly identified as a serious breach of the Counter-Terrorism (Palace of Westminster) Act, prohibiting the expression of any political view critical of the Prime Minister within two kilometres of the House of Commons. All forces within the Met area had been summoned to provide back-up, as central London was cordoned off as part of what was code-named 'Operation Menezes 2'. The suspect was eventually detained and held for 48 hours pending his rendition to Tonbridge Wells, via the Algerian prison system.

2000 hrs Taking advantage of the temporary redeployment of the entire Neasden force to central London, it was decided to resume our monitoring exercise on the World Cup Group Z (Mongolia v. Luxembourg) while partaking of a Chinese dinner in Gerrard Street's fashionable Wei Roo Nee restaurant ('Cantonese tapas at its best'). The following items were consumed: 14, 21, 23, double portion of 32, 45, 78, and 120 bottles of 86.

2400 hrs When the proprietor of the Wei Roo Nee, Mr La La Po, presented his bill he was arrested for exhibiting a white and red flag bearing the legend 'Come On England!', and charged under the Protection of Sensitive Celtic Minorities Act 2006 with displaying an inflammatory racist object.

"NOW you're entitled to use the disabled badge"

MACCA'S NEW BRIDE SHOCK

All you need is ruv

It's the end of an error

Use for an England flag

'WE LOST! SOB SNIFF!'

K.J.L.

'Lions led by donkeys'

by W.W.I. Deedes

It was ninety minutes ago today that our heroic lads lost the greatest battle in world history.

Millions of people wept as they struggled to come to terms with the worst defeat in our island's story.

No one could doubt the courage of those at the front line, those heroic figures who obeyed orders and went unhesitatingly onto the field. But for those leaders like General Sven Haig who orchestrated the catastrophe from the safety of his Soho HQ there can be nothing but ignominy.

Somme Like it Not

His tactics were hopeless and wildly out of date and led directly to defeat. As a famous world cup poet Kenneth Wilfredowenstone wrote at the time, "They think it's all over the top – it is now."

● *On other pages*: Small piece about the First World War, p94.

Wedding of the Century

How They Are Related

Old King Cole	Tweedie Dum
Nat King Cole	Tweedie Dee
Samuel Taylor Cole	Tweedie Pie
John 'Hondootedly' Cole	Sylvester the Cat
Helmut Kohl	Christopher Sylvester
Cole Porter	Jill Tweedie
David Cole-man	Harris Tweedie
Ashley Scoles	Cheryl Baker
Joe Cole	**Cheryl Blair**

GERMANS COMPLAIN ABOUT STEREOTYPING

by Our Foreign Affairs Staff **Jonathan Leake and Basil Fawlty-Water-Towers**

THE British public have been asked to respect German sensitivities and have been told "Don't mention the water!" by senior German executives in charge of British utilities.

Dam Busters

Said one Thames Water manager, Oberwaterführer Von Tap, "We are fed up with your constant references to us losing the water. You Britishers are still obsessed by ze water.

"You must let it go – like us. We let it go everywhere!! Ha Ha! Ha!"

He added, "For you, Tommy ze water is over!!

---

the WORLD C***S

PAUL WOOS

ENGLAND LIMP OUT OF THE WORLD CUP... KILL RONALDO · IT'S PATHETIC...

ONE STAMP... CONTRACT SVEN GORAN ERIKSSON · OFFICIALLY TERMINATED · ENGLAND MANAGER

A WINK... F.A. TROPHY CABINET · SO LONG BOYS! · CHEQUE · AND THEN OFF!

IT'S NOT THE RESULT WE EXPECTED · SVEN £25M · TROPHIES O · FOOTBALL ASSOCIATION

GLENDA JOCKSTRAP

THE EYE'S WORLD CUP WONDERGIRL!

■ HEY MISTER!? Don't blame Sven!!? It's not the super-cool Swede's fault that England's hopes were so cruelly dashed??!? Sven did his best, no man could do more, but when the moment of truth came our lads just weren't good enough!!!? So all hail to The Magnificent Sven, let down by the Unmagnificent Eleven!!?! Geddit??!

■ SVEN??!? What a disgrace!!?! 25 bleedin' million quid we paid the sex-crazed Swede from the land of the smorgasbord!?!! And what's he done for his money??! Swede F.A.!! That's what!? Geddit???! Even my old Gran could have picked a better squad than Sven!!? As for the so-called tactics of the Scandinavian Supershagger – 5-4-1??! Don't make me laugh!!? 9-9-9 would be more like it, Sven, so we could get you banged up in a cell for your criminal incompetence, you sex-mad bespectacled bastard from the land of Bjorn Borg!!?!

■ HEY MISTER!?! Lay off the spud-faced nipper, puh-lease!!? He's only a little scally in short trousers who can't read and write and doesn't know right from wrong!?!! The last thing he needs is for the great British public to crucify him at his moment of agony!!?! So let's all keep Roo-ting for little Wayney (Geddit?!) – his day will come again!!?!

■ WAYNE bloody Rooney!?! Aren't-chasickofhim?!! The spud-faced loser who can't even control his temper, let alone the ball?! You may have broken your metatarsal – shame you didn't break your legs – and your arms – and your neck!!?! Geddit?!! Metatarsal??! Mega-Arsehole more like it?!

■ SHED A TEAR if you will for the ex-England skipper!!?! He gave his all in his country's hour of need!!? Don't blame David – it's not his fault he was picked by the sex-crazed smorgasbord-guzzler from the land of Abba?! As he goes a-creepin' and a-weepin' into the sunset, I say "God bless you, Dave, and your beautiful wife and lovely kiddies!?!!"

■ BEND IT like Beckham?!? *END* it like Beckham, more like – i.e. in tears again!!? Dead ball specialist?!? Dead beat is closer to it!!? Good riddance to the big girl's blouse with his anoxeric wife and stupidly named kids!?! Go back to Madrid and get yourself a new tattoo saying "Loser" on your forehead!?! (Geddit??!)

■ PENALTY SHOOT-OUT?! They should *all* be shot!?! Except for Hargreaves, who's German anyway!?! All together now – "Deutschland Deutschland Über Alles!" *(Is this right? Ed.)*

■ NO WONDER we lost!?! Look at the ref!?! He was an Argie, for God's sake!!?! Of course he rigged the match in favour of the Portuguese!?! We won the Falklands, didn't we, so he's hardly going to let us win the World Cup!?!! Gotcha Señor!!?! Or we will do if you ever show your face around here again!!?!

■ CHRISTIANO RONALDO!?! More like 'Judas' Ronaldo!?!! We saw you a-blinkin' and a-winkin' at the crowd when you got the filthy Argie ref to send off the hot-headed spud-faced nipper who was picked by the sex-crazed Swedish love machine *(I'm showing you the yellow card. Ed.).*

■ GOD!?! What a disgrace!?!! Millions of Britons prayed to you as our lads queued up to take their penalties!?! And whose side were you on?!? Thank God you don't exist, so we don't have to believe in you any more!?! (Right that's it – red card. Ed.)

RECYCLING CENTRE

WORLD CUP WALL CHARTS

Alternative History, Dunkirk. May 1940

YOU ARE CURRENTLY BEING HELD IN A QUEUE. PLEASE WAIT UNTIL ONE OF OUR OPERATIVES IS FREE.

Nursery Times

July 7, 2006

PRINCE CHARMING 'WORTH EVERY PENNY'

by Our Royal Staff **Mother O'Goose**

FAIRYLAND was thrown into a state of uproar yesterday following the publication of Prince Charming's household accounts.

Last year, it was revealed, the Prince cost each man, woman, fairy, gnome and goblin in the kingdom half a silver sixpence.

The money goes to support the Prince's lavish lifestyle, involving the throwing of a continual round of balls, requiring the services of hundreds of footmen, butlers, mice and pumpkins.

At the Prince's country residence, Highgrove Castle, a chef is permanently employed in making the Prince's favourite blackbird pie.

A palace spokesman said,

"The Prince represents very good value – particularly since he married the Ugly Sister, who requires very little upkeep compared with the late Cinderella, Princess of Hearts."

Furthermore, the Prince's latest venture, selling organic Duchy Gingerbread Men, has generated a large amount of revenue, namely 1p.

● Full story and details of accounts **94**

77

BLAIR'S SECRET PAST
New Shock

> I believe in Marx

> So do I... their underpants are so comfortable

That Blair Letter To Michael Foot In Full

IN 1982 the young Tony Blair sat down and wrote a 900-page letter to the then Labour leader, Michael Foot. The letter was carefully preserved in a dustbin for 25 years and has only now come to light when it was found on a rubbish tip in Hampstead. Now read on...

Dear Mr Foot,

It was a great privilege and honour to meet you and to be given a copy of your marvellous and brilliant book *My Heroes*. It was fascinating to read about all these people you know so much about. Nye Hazlitt, Tom Bevan, Jim Payne and, of course, Dave Spart. Wow! Socialism! It really blew my mind. And what about Karl Marx! What a beard! What a guy! You know, reading your book really made me think that these cool men might be onto something important.

You know, I agree with everything that Marx says, and also what you say about Marx and also what he says about you... *(The letter continues in a similar vein for over 20,000 words before reaching its conclusion...)* In short, Mr Foot, sir, your brilliant and wonderful book has really made me think about all kinds of things, but principally about how much I would like to be given a winnable seat so that I can get into power and destroy the Labour Party. Only joking, Mr Foot, sir!

Yours,

Comrade Tony Blair

"He's a very good gardener... and, of course, there's all the manure"

THE SUN SAYS

LOCK UP THE PAEDO PLAYWRIGHT!

Why is this monster free to roam the theatres of New York? He has been found guilty of writing a sick play about a molester of under-age boys.

Yet is this fiend behind bars where he belongs?

No! He has been allowed to "pick up" no fewer than six innocent Tonys on seedy Broadway!

How perverted can you get?

The Sun says: "It's time 'Bennett the Bespectacled Beast' was made History, Boys!?!

> WHAT'S THE MEANING OF LIFE?

> ABOUT 5 YEARS

EXCLUSIVE TO THE DAILY MAIL

Non-Story About M&S Which Means We Can Run A Picture Of A Model In Her Bra And Knickers

DAILY MAIL editor Paul Dacre today confirmed that his newspaper would be reprinting an M&S press release so that the paper could accompany it with a picture of a model in her bra and knickers.

On Other Pages

Vitriolic attack on men who view sleazy internet porn accompanied by sleazy photo of a woman in a bra and suspenders **23**

Story of Java earthquake accompanied by photo of tearful survivor in her M&S bra and panties **39**

HEWITT LAUNCHES BREATHING PACK

by Our Health Staff **Annie State**

HEALTH SECRETARY Patricia Hewitt yesterday unveiled her new £2 billion campaign to "get Britain breathing".

In a leaflet to be issued to every household in the country, Ms Hewitt lays down new guidelines which she believes could save millions of lives every year.

"Breathing is probably the most important thing in all our lives. And yet no one is given any help in how to do it."

A video to be issued with the pamphlet demonstrates, with the aid of animated figures based on the Teletubbies, how every one of us can benefit from breathing.

Says Ms Hewitt "it only takes a few minutes to read the leaflet and watch the video – and yet it can make all the difference between life and death."

The leaflet sets out detailed, easy-to-follow instructions on how to breathe in, and equally to breathe out. It underlines the dangers of holding one's breath for too long, or even of forgetting to breathe at all.

The leaflet entitled "Breathing – A Strategy for Survival" is published by the Government Publications Agency (formerly Her Majesty's Stationery Office).

FORMER LEADER SPEAKS OUT

The Labour Party has never believed in selection by ability

TEACHER 'TEACHES PUPIL' SHOCK

THE EDUCATION Department has reacted angrily today after it was revealed that a teacher at a school in Britain had actually been teaching her pupils.

"Surely she should have been having sex with them or getting them to set their own exams, or getting knifed by them."

"People like this have no place in the teaching profession", said a Department (cont. p. 94)

"School trophies aren't what they once were"

New from Royal Mail

A special commemorative set of stamps to celebrate British achievement in the field of serial killings.

Great Serial Killers
Myra Hindley

Great Serial Killers
Harold Shipman

Great Serial Killers
Dennis Nilsen

Great Serial Killers
Fred & Rosemary West

Throughout history Britain has led the world in producing some of the greatest names in multiple homicide and we at Royal Mail are proud to offer this unique collection for a very reasonable sum of £526.

Send now to: Royal Mail, Serial Killer Set Offer, Mount Unpleasant, London WC1.
Please allow 28 years for delivery.

THE TALIBAN
An Apology

IN COMMON with all other newspapers we may have given the impression that we regarded the Taliban as "a spent force", following their defeat at the hands of the United States and British forces in 2001. Headlines such as "They think it's all Omar", "Goodbye to the Taliban!" and "Burqua off, Beardies!" may have led readers to believe that the Taliban were no longer a credible threat to the stability of the region and that only small pockets of resistance remained to be "mopped up". We now realise that the Taliban are the greatest danger to world peace in human history (apart from al Qaeda, obviously) and are capable of putting hundreds of thousands of trained fighters into the field, making our own soldiers extremely vulnerable to attack, humiliation and death. Recent headlines, including "Bring back our boys", "Time to retreat" and "Run for your life, it's the Taliban" will have made our new position clear. We would like to apologise to the Taliban unreservedly for any confusion that our previous articles may have caused.

Let's Parlez Franglais!

Lesson 94 l'Apologie avec Zizou Zidane

Zizou *(pour c'est lui)*:
Naturellement je regrette beaucoup si mon 'head-butt' dans le World Cup (devant dix billion de viewers dans leur fauteils autour de la entire monde) est un mauvais example for les kiddies. Mais, franchement, je ne regrette rien et je refuse totalement de faire un apologie a ce batard Maserati, qui est un bit of un poof, excusez mon francais!

M. Le President Chirac *(parce que c'est lui)*: Mon brave, vous êtes le plus grand Frenchman dans notre histoire (sauf que moi, naturellement). Acceptez la legion d'honneur premiere classe. Vous êtes un vrai role model pour tous les kiddies francaises, noir et blanc, riche et pauvre, les Chrêtiens et les Moslems comme vous qui set fire aux banlieus de Paris chaque semaine....

Zizou: Voici un head-butt for you, M. le President, aussi. *(BIFF)*

Chirac: Ouch! Vive la France! À bas les Eyeties!

DAILY GNOME EXCLUSIVE

Revealed: the insult that made Zinedine Zidane see red in the world cup final

THE Daily Gnome can exclusively reveal exactly what was said to the French captain that led to him head-butting the Italian defender Marco Materazzi.

"A lip-reading expert consulted by the Daily Gnome is certain Zidane was told 'Sven Goran Eriksson says you are good enough to play in the England team'.

"No wonder he flipped his lid."

MAXIMUS, YOU LOST. HOW'S IT FEEL?

I'M GUTTED

Post-gladitorial sports interviews

'WE WERE WRONG ABOUT EVERYTHING' ADMITS BLAIR

by Our Political Staff **Peter O'Bore**

THE PRIME Minister last night launched an unprecedented attack on the Government, describing all its policies as **"complete rubbish"**.

"Let's start," he said, "with ID Cards. What a farce that idea has turned out to be! Whoever came up with that one should be ashamed of themselves.

"Merging the police forces? Did you ever hear anything so daft in your life?

"Human Rights Act? What a load of liberal, lefty rubbish!

"Home Information Packs? A completely crackpot scheme – even an idiot could see that wouldn't work."

When Mr Blair was asked whether there was anything he was in favour of, he replied, "Yes, of course. Nuclear power, Marvellous. Can't get enough of it. Gifted children? Why shouldn't they have their own schools? Mrs Thatcher? Don'tchaloveher? She should have a State Funeral, no question. Best prime minister we've had since myself."

At this point, two parliamentary advisers in white coats escorted Mr Blair to a quiet room, where he was later reported to be "in an unstable condition".

OLD JOKES REVISITED

As told by Tara Palmer-Tomkinson's dog.

Dog: I say, I say, I say! My owner's got no nose.

Man: How does she smell?

Dog: Heavily of cocaine.

FRIEND OF THE ROYALS IN NOSE SHOCK

I blame Charlie

New Words

Woss *(n. vulg)* an act of self-abuse or onanism. Example: "He was caught by the headmaster having a woss" (2006)

Wosser *(n. slang)* abusive term to describe interviewer being paid millions of pounds a year to work for the BBC. Example: "Did you see that bloke on TV on Friday night – what a total wosser!" (2006)

Cameron *(n.)* person stupid enough to go on show presented by wosser *(see above)* to answer questions about having a woss *(That's enough new words. Ed.)*

POETRY CORNER

In Memoriam Slobodan Milosevic and Humphrey the Cat

So. Farewell then
Serbian tyrant and
Number Ten
Pet.

You both occupied the
Seats of power
And were responsible
For many
Deaths.

The one of Bosnians,
Croatians, Kosovans etc.
The other
Of mice and
Robins.

Though both of you
Claimed to be
Innocent
(Except Humphrey).

    E.J. Serb (17½ thousand dead)

Lines written on the appointment of Miss Kirsty Young to become the presenter of Desert Island Discs

So. Hullo then
Kirsty Young.
You have been chosen
To present
Desert Island
Discs.

"What is your next
Record?"
That will be your
Catchphrase. "And
Your luxury item?"
That will be
Another.

All together now.
Da-da-da-di-dum
Di-da-da
Di-dum-dum
Swoosh, swoosh,
Squawk, squawk.

    E.J. Thribb (17½)

A podcast of the above poem, read by Stephen Fry, can be down-loaded from www.getsverse.com

---

MODERN NURSERY RHYMES

Little Zak Horner
Sat in the corner,
Eating his Christmas pie.
When told not to eat
And go back to his seat,
He told teacher to fuck off
        and die.

Mary had a little lamb
It and she were buddies
It followed her to school
        and got
An A in media studies

Ring-a-ring-a-roses,
We've all got cirrhosis

Lines on the death of Lord Lichfield, photographer and cousin of the Queen

So. Farewell
Then Lord
Lichfield,

Photographer
Royal.

"Watch the
Birdie, Your
Royal Highness!"

That was
Your catchphrase.

"Say cheese,
Ma'am."

That was another.
    E.J. Thribb (17½)

In Memoriam Harry 'Toppo' Thompson, TV Producer, Biographer and Novelist

So. Farewell
Then Harry
'Toppo' Thompson.

Yes you were
The producer
Of many famous
Comedy shows.

*Have I Got
News For
You. Enfield
And Chums. Ali G.*

And of
Course *They
Think It's
All Over.*

Sadly, it is
Now.
    E.J. Thribb (17½)

Lines on the impending divorce of Sir Mark Thatcher and Ms Diana Bergdorf

So. Farewell
Then the marriage
Of Mrs Thatcher's
Only son
And Diana Bergdorf,
Daughter of a
Texan millionaire
Car dealer.

She was a
Good catch
For the wayward
Baronet.

But eventually she'd
Had enough and
Bergerd-orf.
    E.J. Thribb (17½)

New-look Enid Blyton
Noddy & The Gnome Secretary

BIG EARS was angry. "Noddy has lost his sense of purpose and direction," he told everyone in Toytown. "He shouldn't be allowed to drive the car any more."

Poor Noddy was sad at this. "I thought you were my friend, Big Ears. After all, I gave you a lift in my car."

"Yes, but then you threw me out of the car," said Big Ears, getting really red in the face, which made his big ears look even bigger.

"That's because you let all the goblins roam around Toytown, stealing people's sixpences," said Noddy crossly, "you bitter and useless *(Continued p. 94)*

That Honorary Degree Citation In Full

SALUTAMUS GUILLIEMUS CONNOLLIUS COMEDIANUS CALEDONENSIS APPELLATUS MAGNUS YINNUS NATO IN GORBALIBUS LABORIO NAUTICO CONSTRUCTIONEM MAESTRO BANJOENSIS LUDENTUM CUM BARBUM MULTICOLORUM RIDICULOSUM ET ACCENTIUS GLASWEGIANUS IMPENETRABILE SED FREQUENTER APPARATIO IN PROGRAMMUS TELEVISUALIS PARKINSONIUS CUM MULTI JOCULARI CRUDUS PER EXEMPLO 'FARTUM' 'BUMMEN' 'WILLYIUM' ET CETERA ET CETERA. MARITUS AD PAMELAM STEVENSONIAM COMEDIANA ANTIPODEANA ET SUBSEQUENTER PSYCHOTHERAPISTICUM DRIVELLIANA IN CALIFORNIA IN NOVO MUNDO SED POST HAEC TRIUMPHES NIHIL IMPORTANTUS EXCEPTIONE ADVERTUS PISSPORRUS PER LOTTO NATIONALE CUM SLOGANO PISSPOORIS-SIMO 'NON VIVO PARVO, VIVO LOTTO'. GAUDEAMUS!

© The Royal Scottish Academy Of Music And Drama, Glasgow (formerly Mrs McNaughtie's School Of Elocution And Deportment, over McHackey's Chippie, 231a Sauchiehall Street – "Scotch Tapas At Its Best".

Eye 10 Best Buys No. 94 Bath Plugs

1. 'The Pluggo' from Asda. Basic 'fit for purpose' plug. Iconic design. Fits any bath. Made in Vietnam. 22p. *Best Economy Buy.*

2. 'The Chatsworth' from the Gloucestershire Bath Co., Cirencester. Exact replica of plug designed for the 4th Duke of Devonshire by Sir Joseph Paxton. £978.99. *Best Luxury Buy.*

3. 'The Planet Saver' from Body Shop. These eco-friendly, biodegradable plugs are specially designed to dissolve in water. £25 for packet of 100. *Best Organic Buy.*

4. 'De Pløgge' Ikea have entered the bath-plug market with an exciting range of plugs in many colours that you can assemble yourself. From all Ikea branches. £9.99. *Best Bargain Buy.*

5. 'The Poseidon XP-15.' Specially designed by NASA scientists for use in the space shuttle – is made from titanium and will last for 10 million years. £2 million. *Best Value for Money. (That's enough plugs. Ed.)*

DAILY HIS-TORYGRAPH

Friday, July 21, 2006

Sheriff Of Notting Hill In Policy U-Turn

by Will "Scarlet" Deedes

IN AN astonishing reversal of traditional Conservative thinking, the Sheriff of Notting Hill has called for society

to be more understanding towards Robin Hoodie.

The Men In Green

"What Hoodie needs is love and compassion, not being hunted through the forest and hung from the nearest tree."

Sir David of Cameron continued: "Sure, Hoodie goes around breaking the law, stealing from the rich and frightening the elderly as they travel around Middle England.

"But it's no good outlawing Hoodie and trying to ban him from shopping centres in Notting Hill.

"Instead, we've got to make him feel included in our society. After all, men in suits of armour probably seem pretty threatening to him."

Sheriff Cameron is 39.

"Hug that thief!"

KEIRA WOWS FANS AT PIRATES PREMIERE

YES, Keira Knightley looked fabulous last night as she posed for pictures on the red carpet!

The star of the new 'Pirates Of The Caribbean' blockbuster happily chatted to fans and signed autographs at the glittering opening of the movie phenomenon of the year.

However, lovely Keira did confess that she had a weight problem. "Maybe I need to lose a few pounds," she laughed, as *(cont. p. 94)*

BUSH – NEW MIDDLE EAST ROAD MAP

There's Nothing Wrong With Lads Mags

by Former Editor of 'Huge Jugs' SEBASTIAN BLOKEY

HOW dare Labour MP Claire Curtis-Thomas suggest that lads mags should be placed on the top shelf in newsagents as they are little more than pornography?

Surely she can see that "lads mags" differ significantly from "porn mags" because they have an incredible sense of humour.

For instance, I once accompanied a picture of two topless women licking ice cream off each other's breasts with the caption "Just one more Horn-etto!". No doubt Clare-sad-old-lesbian must be one of those bunny boilers with far too much facial hair and an arse the size of the back end of a bus, to appreciate "lads mags" sly and subversive sense of humour.

Far from being porn, "lads mags" in fact celebrate women with breasts of all shapes and sizes… as long as the hooters in question are flipping enormous.

The Book of Ehud

Chapter 94

1. And it came to pass in the days when Ehud ruled the Land of Israel as Sharon lay sleeping in an coma that the Hamas-ites came privily by night and stole from the Israelites a soldier whose name was Shalit and led him away into captivity.

2. And Ehud counselled himself thus, saying.

3. "What shall I do? Shall I smite the Hamas-ites like unto Sharon? Or smite them an hundredfold also like unto Sharon?".

4. And he decided to go for the hundredfold option.

5. And so he sayeth unto the Children of Israel, "Gird up thy tanks and go forth into the Land of Gaza and smite everything you see until this captive is restored to us."

6. And they did even as Ehud commanded.

7. But, guesseth what? The captured soldier returneth not.

8. And, meanwhile, there was great wailing and gnashing of teeth in the Land of Gaza, which was turned into an wilderness fit only for the cockatrice and the ant.

9. Now there dwelt in the Land of Lebanon certain Hizboll-ites who did look upon the works of the Hamas-ites and sayeth one to another:

10. "What the Hamas-ites have done, let us do also. For it seemeth an good idea.

11. "For as sure as the noonday sun riseth over the Cedars of Lebanon, the Sons of Israel will be consumed by wrath and their judgement will leaveth from the window."

12. And it was even as the Hizboll-ites foretold.

13. They also crept privily by night (see-eth above) and led certain soldiers of Israel into captivity.

14. Then Ehud waxed exceeding wroth, like unto the hornet when a man whacketh it with his flip-flop.

15. And Ehud again took counsel with himself (see-eth above again).

16. And, lo, yet again he reasoned that smiting was the only answer, but this time it would be an thousandfold.

17. So he commanded the Israelites: "Go forth unto the Land of Lebanon and lay it waste like unto Gaza, except more so, for these people learneth not their lesson.

18. "Unlike myself."

19. And so it came to pass and the Israelites smote the Hizboll-ites, and they smote back at the cities of the Israelites and meanwhile the Hamas-ites did some smiting as well.

20. And the Hamas-ites and Hizboll-ites rejoiced, saying "It worketh every time."

21. But Ehud hearkeneth not, and sayeth unto himself:

22. "Perhaps I should extend the smiting to the Syrian-ites and then the Iran-ites and all the rest of the Arab-ites.

23. "Until there is no one left to smite.

24. "And then the children of Israel may dwell in peace. Just as our forefathers didn't."

(To be continued throughout history)

The Daily Telegraph

Cash for Honours Scandal

The news that Lord Levy has been arrested in connection with the Labour loan inquiry raises profoundly disturbing questions about the role of the Prime Minister and Ha Ha Ha Ha Ha Ha Ha Ha Ha Ha Ha Ha Ha Ha Ha

© The Daily Telegraph

MY DINNER WITH LORD LEVY

by Dominic Lawson

I was lucky enough to be invited to dinner by Lord Levy who is a very nice man and very important! He has a big house with lots of nice things in it. And they're all white. Amazing!

Anyway there were lots of really important people at the dinner party as well as myself.

There was the Head of MI5, the Governor of the Bank of England, the Archbishop of Canterbury (I think or maybe it was the Duke of Kent), the First Lord of the Admiralty, Sir David Frost and Lord Rees-Mogg.

It was really interesting and then guess what? The telephone rang and Lord Levy answered it, whispering to us: "It's Tony". Everyone was most impressed. Imagine the Prime Minister ringing up a party where I was, surrounded by famous people. Surely that is proof that Lord Levy is innocent?

© Read Dominic Lawson only in the Independent, the Mail and everywhere else.

ADVERTISEMENT

CLASSIC DVDs FROM GNOME

FIDDLER ON THE PRISON ROOF

starring
Topol as Lord Levy
with the unforgettable hit song:
*"If you were a rich man
Would you like a peerage?"*

ORDER YOUR COPY NOW!

EXCLUSIVE TO PRIVATE EYE

That Ghulam Noon Loan Form In Full

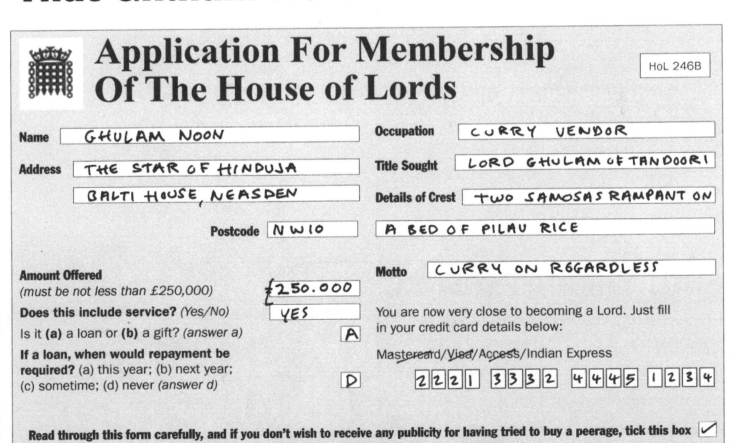

Application For Membership Of The House of Lords

HoL 246B

Name GHULAM NOON

Address THE STAR OF HINDUJA

BALTI HOUSE, NEASDEN

Postcode NW10

Amount Offered
(must be not less than £250,000) £250.000

Does this include service? *(Yes/No)* YES

Is it **(a)** a loan or **(b)** a gift? *(answer a)* A

If a loan, when would repayment be required? (a) this year; (b) next year; (c) sometime; (d) never *(answer d)* D

Occupation CURRY VENDOR

Title Sought LORD GHULAM OF TANDOORI

Details of Crest TWO SAMOSAS RAMPANT ON

A BED OF PILAU RICE

Motto CURRY ON REGARDLESS

You are now very close to becoming a Lord. Just fill in your credit card details below:

Mastercard/Visa/Access/Indian Express

2221 3332 4445 1234

Read through this form carefully, and if you don't wish to receive any publicity for having tried to buy a peerage, tick this box ✓

Then send completed form in plain brown envelope to:
Government Peerage Offer, c/o Lord Levy, 10 Downing Street, London SW1

THE BOOK OF EHUD

Chapter 94: *The Smighty Warriors Go Forth*

1. And lo, it came to pass that Ehud sent the mighty warriors of Israel, the sons and even the daughters of Israel, indeed all the children of Israel who could carry a sword or ride in an chariot of iron, into the land of Le-ban-on.

2. And Ehud spake unto the children of Israel in this wise: O children of Israel, the time hath come for the smiting that will end all smiting.

3. For too many years the Hez-boll-ites have been an thorn in our flesh, like unto the scorpion that creepeth up in the night and stingeth a man in his foot, yea, even before he can lay his hand upon the flip-flop beneath his bed in order to smite it dead.

4. Talking of which, Ehud concluded, it is time for some serious smiting, even the final day of reckoning with the Hez-boll-ites.

5. Ye are to go into the land of the cedars of Lib-anus and smite all that moveth – not just the Hez-boll-ites but also the Leb-anites (who may be no friends to the Hez-boll-ites but that is just the luck that is called tough) and indeed anyone else who getteth in our way.

6. And the children of Israel saith unto themselves, yea, it will all be over in seven days.

7. And it will be like unto an piece of cake.

8. So the warriors of Israel went forth into the land of Leb-an-on to do as they had been commanded by Ehud, the son of Sharon.

9. But, lo, it was not as it had been foretold by Ehud.

10. For the Hez-boll-ites had hidden themselves privily, in caves and holes in the ground, like unto the cunning fox which concealeth itself by day and, when night comes, jumpeth out and fireth an rocket at Haifa.

11. And so it was with the Hez-boll-ites. And the children of Israel found themselves on the receiving end of the smiting, for an change.

12. And in the streets of Haifa there was much wailing and gnashing of teeth.

13. For many had been slain, even men, women and children.

14. Though not as many as the Leb-anites, men, women and children, who had been slain by the sons of Israel.

15. And so it continueth for six days. And on the seventh day Ehud looked upon what he had done and said, "This is not good."

16. And he cried aloud, cursing the Hez-boll-ites with an mighty curse, saying, "This goeth not according to plan.

17. "So now it is time for the plan that is called B – that is to say more smiting."

18. And where Ehud had smote an hundred-fold, he now smote an thousand-fold, even the cities of Tyre and Sidon, and many others too numerous to mention (but they are all named in the Bible).

19. And among those who were smitten were the sons of Un, who are called the makers of peace.

20. But, lo, the Hez-boll-ites were still there, like unto the nettle of the desert which, the more it is cut down, the more it groweth up to sting again.

21. And the children of Israel muttereth among themselves, saying, "Verily this Ehud hath been put to the test and hath been found sorely wanting.

22. "For even Sharon, who sleepeth like unto one who is dead, would make a better fist of it."

23. And Ehud took counsel with himself, asking what he should now do.

24. What, he asketh, would Sharon have done if he were standing in my shoes?

25. And the answer cameth to him as follows: "I know – all that is needed is more smiting."

Chapter 95: *The Miracle at Qana*

1. And lo, it came to pass that in the town of Qana which is in Galilee there were many Leban-ites, women and children, gathered together in one dwelling, for they had taken refuge there and they were sore afraid..

2. And they had good reason.

3. For Ehud sent out his flying weapons by night and smote them all, even as they slept.

4. And all the children of Israel were amazed and cried out, "Verily, this is the Miracle at Qana. Ehud hath turned living people into dead ones."

(Continued until the end of the world)

SPOT THE DIFFERENCE

A Handy Guide For Israeli Soldiers

THE UN	HEZBOLLAH
Brings humanitarian aid to region	Brings rocket launchers to region
Helps those caught up in terror	A terrorist organisation
Determined to find a peaceful solution	Determined to bomb Israel to smithereens
Hated by US and targeted by Israeli rockets	Hated by US and targeted by Israeli rockets

SURGICAL STRIKE

HISTORIC MIDDLE EAST AGREEMENT

"We're agreed"

"Israel can do whatever it likes"

Advertisement

From August 21st, post will be priced by size as well as weight. We're changing the way we make money. This is how it will work.

Small amount of money

Large amount of money

Huge packet of money

Royal Mail **Delivering 1st Class profits to ourselves**

New Words

Incident *(n.)* large-scale massacre of innocent people, e.g. "We deeply regret this unfortunate incident" (Israeli spokesman, 2006).

Disproportionate *(adj.)* unsuitable, excessive, a bit much, e.g. "The dropping of a nuclear weapon by Israel is in no way disproportionate" (US spokesman, 2006).

Diplomacy *(n.)* not talking to people you don't like, e.g. "We are engaging in diplomacy with Syria and Iran" (Condoleezza Rice, 2006).

BLAIR DENIAL

"I'm not George Bush's poodle – I'm Rupert Murdoch's"

SCHOOLS NO LONGER TO TEACH THE DIFFERENCE BETWEEN 'RIGHT AND LEFT'

by Our Political Staff **Art A. Tack**

THERE was outrage today at a government decision to scrap the section of the National Curriculum which compels schools to teach children the difference between right and left.

However a spokesman for the ministry of education hit back at critics.

"In today's society children make up their own minds about what is so-called 'right' and what is left."

Confidence Trick

"We have moved on from the old-fashioned idea that you tell children that there is some sort of absolute distinction between these two opposing concepts. Both are equally valid."

He concluded, "As long as children are confident and secure in the *(cont. p94.)*

A Taxi Driver writes

EVERY week a well-known cab driver is invited to comment on an issue of topical importance. This week: **Polly Toynbee** (Cab No. 2468).

Blimey, guv, these immigrants flooding into Britain from every corner of the globe. Don't get me wrong. I'm no racist. I've got nothing against foreigners coming over here and taking our jobs. Good luck to them, I say. But let's face it, this is only a tiny island when you come to look at it. I mean all these what they call "Eastern Europeans" – Poles, Latvians, and now the government, are giving the green light to millions of Bulgarians. I mean take this traffic jam we're sitting in it's solid all the way up to Marble Arch. I guarantee that at least half come from overseas. Oi, you lot, get off the bloody road! Whoever's to blame for it should be strung up. I had that Enoch Powell in the back of my cab many years ago. Very clever man.

Next week: Jim Sheridan MSP writes in praise of the jury system.

HIGH STREET

ENGLISH SPOKEN HERE

MIKE TURNER

HOW I WOULD SOLVE ALL THE WORLD'S PROBLEMS

by Tory leader **David Cameron**

PEOPLE keep asking me what I would do about the war in the Middle East.

Well, I've got one simple answer. We could start by saving water when we brush our teeth.

The only thing which matters in the world today is that we save the planet for future generations.

And it's up to each and every one of us to make a contribution.

Do you realise, for example. that if everyone in the country turned off their television sets at night, we would save enough electricity to light a city the size of Birmingham?

Just think about it.

And here's another thought.

If all businesses provided bedrooms for their staff, then no one would need to go home at night.

Not only would this produce a massive saving in the cars and trains which would no longer be needed to get people to and from work.

If people weren't at home in the evenings, they wouldn't need to turn on their television sets at all – thus saving enough electricity to light and heat a country the size of Africa!

So there you are.

Let's make a start today in building the world of tomorrow!

© *David Cameron 2006.*

SPOT THE DIFFERENCE

PRINCESS DIANA	HEATHER MILLS
● Statuesque blonde hounded by tabloids	● Statuesque blonde hounded by tabloids
● Campaigned against landmines	● Campaigned against landmines
● Represented by Anthony Julius in messy divorce	● Represented by Anthony Julius in messy divorce
● Married Charlie	● Married right Charlie

BRITAIN IS NOW 'HOTTER THAN THE SURFACE OF THE SUN'

by Our Credulous Correspondent **A.A. Gullible**

"BRITAIN is now hotter than the surface of the sun," bored scientists claimed yesterday.

"It's true," said one boffin, stifling giggles. "We've tested it and everything. You can put it in your newspaper if you like, next to the one about humans being descended from rocks, disco-dancing bees, and how cheese makes you invisible.

"If the current weather continues," he said, smirking, "we may have to feed you that one about dinosaurs being able to read and write."

Eye Summer Quiz

Our picture is of the new logo of the Conservative Party. But what does it represent? Is it:

A. A floral hat as worn by Camilla, Duchess of Cornwall, at this year's Royal Ascot race meeting?

B. A controlled nuclear explosion at the Khomeini testing range in Iran?

C. A burst water main in Sutton High Street which Thames Water has not repaired in 15 years?

Get the right answer and you could be the Tory candidate for Mayor of London.

CHILD SUPPORT AGENCY TO BE SCRAPPED

by Our Political Staff **Peter O'Bore**

THE government yesterday announced that it is to abolish the ill-fated Child Support Agency, which for the past 13 years has been in charge of forcing absent parents to pay for their children's upkeep.

The CSA is to be replaced by a new body, the ACS (the Agency for Child Support), which will have responsibility for forcing absent parents to pay for their children's upkeep.

The CSA's 8,000 employees will all be transferred to the new agency.

Said a spokesman, "This is a radical new departure for the government. We have had the courage to admit that the CSA has been a complete disaster, but we are confident that we can rectify things by reassigning all their responsibilities to the new agency.

"What's really important," he went on, "is that none of the staff should be given the SAC."

THE WEEK IN PICTURES

Taking the Peace

Ready, Aim... Ceasefire!

Old Jokes Revisited

Do you know how to sort out the Middle East?

No, but you hum it and I'll pick it up

Bush Mercy Mission

Don't worry son. You'll soon be well enough to go and die for your country

MADE IN ISRAEL

NICHOLAS

as the rockets by-passed the local hospital and the children's nursery and instead slammed directly into a Hezbollah rocket launcher," said one astonished local. "No one could quite believe that we weren't seeing a sickening loss of innocent lives."

Israel promised a full investigation into the incident, but insisted that since the conflict had started only a tiny proportion of their rockets had hit their intended targets.

Day 94

ISRAELI ROCKETS 'HIT HEZBOLLAH TARGET'

ISRAELI government officials last night refused to confirm eye-witness reports that two Israeli rockets had actually hit Hezbollah targets in the Southern Lebanese city of Tyre.

"I watched in stunned disbelief

HEZBOLLAH ROCKETS 'HIT SOMETHING'

HEZBOLLAH officials last night refused to confirm eye-witness reports that a Hezbollah rocket had actually hit something in Israel.

Said a spokesman for the Shi'ite militia, "We're launching hundreds of these things every day, hoping to hit innocent civilians and most of the time we miss completely, so Israel gets all the credit for killing women and children which *(cont. p. 94)*

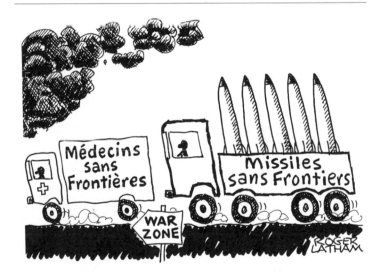

Médecins sans Frontières

Missiles sans Frontiers

WAR ZONE

ROGER LATHAM

THAT LEBANON AGREEMENT IN FULL

1. The state of Israel and the army of Hezbollah do hereby solemnly agree...

2. ...that we want to carry on killing each other.

3. Er...

4. That's it.

Duchess of Love

by DAME SYLVIE KRIN, author of *La Dame Aux Camillas, Heir of Sorrows*, and *Born To Be Queen Consort.*

THE STORY SO FAR: Charles has decided to make some household economies in the interests of combating global warming.

Now read on...

CHARLES was emptying the last of his carefully saved bath water onto his organic purple nanciastors.

"There you go, little fellows. Daddy's giving you a nice, long drink and helping to save the planet at the same time."

The July sun was beating down mercilessly on the parched lawns and herbacious borders of Highgrove.

Charles took off his battered panama hat and fanned his sweating brow.

He called across to Camilla, who was sheltering under a giant-leaved burberry tree, as she struggled to complete the Quick Sudoku puzzle in the Daily Express.

"I've never known it as hot as this," he gasped. "It's this whole fossil fuel thingie. We've all got to play our part in reducing our carbon footprint. Did you know that..."

Camilla frowned, as Charles appeared to be embarking on what had become a familiar theme of their conversations.

"Chazza, can't you see I'm trying to concentrate here. Damn, I've got two fives in one row, and it's all your fault."

It wasn't just the roses that were wilting in the unaccustomed heat.

Camilla felt her own thermometer rising near the top of the scale, yet Charles seemed oblivious.

"You don't seem to understand, Cammers, old girl, this really is the most important issue thingie confronting the human race. I mean, every one of us has got to make cut-backs."

An exhausted squirrel fell out of the tree above his head, and dragged itself into a nearby dubya bush.

"You see, this whole Gaia thingie is going to collapse unless we do something pretty drastic – and I've been looking through the accounts with Sir Alan, and there's a bit of a question mark over your house."

Camilla threw down her newspaper.

"Oh, bugger it, Chazza, that's four fives in a row you've made me do now."

Camilla tore herself away from her beloved Sudoku, and focused her attention on what her husband had just been saying. What was that about her house, her beloved retreat, nestling in the sleepy Wiltshire Weald?

"You see," said Charles, pouring out a glass of fresh, warm rainwater for himself from a traditional-style plastic water butt, "we've got a lot of houses – Highgrove, Clarence House, that one in Scotland... Dunthingie, not to mention all mater's houses.

"When you think how much electricity they all use, you know, millions of kilo-thingies, we've really got to start economising somewhere – and your house is the obvious one to begin with."

Camilla bristled. "Why *my* house? Why not one of *your* ghastly piles? All those huge, dark rooms, full of stags' heads and paintings of your dreary relatives.

"And your granny's place is a nightmare. Open any of the cupboards and a load of empty gin bottles fall out on your head."

"Now hang on," Charles interrupted, his face reddening with anger.

"That's no way to talk about Her Late Majesty, Queen Elizabeth the Queen Mother. I mean, you are a full member of the Royal Family now. There is a sort of, you know, dignity that goes with..."

At that moment the peace of the garden was shattered by the screaming brakes of the Royal People Carrier, as Prince Harry arrived back with 17 of his scantily-clad friends from an evening's dancing and dining at Slappers in Tetbury.

"It's alright," he reassured his companions, as they fell out of the vehicle and stumbled across the flower beds, "Dad's got stacks of booze in the cellar. Follow me, guys, and we'll get stuck in!"

"Cool!" chorused his friends enthusiastically, as the convivial party disappeared into the recesses of the house. Charles, meanwhile, resumed his dissertation on the perils of global warming and the need to conserve energy supplies. "As I was saying, you never turn off the lights and..."

But he might as well have conserved his own energy.

For, as he spoke, Camilla was already at the wheel of her Materazzi Convertible, accelerating down the drive, the wind in her hair and her spirits soaring in line with the speedometer.

Highgrove was behind her and the road ahead stretched towards Little Bedding, her cherished Wiltshire bolthole.

It may be just a humble little cottage, with its 14 bedrooms, swimming pool and stabling for 15 horses. But it was hers, hers, hers... and no one, but no one, was going to take it from her.

© *The Sylvie Krin, 'Stansted Airport Departure Lounge Collection'.*

BETJEMAN AT 100

New Poem Discovered

The flags are flying in the sun,
A happy day for everyone!
  Special programmes on the telly,
  Introduced by old George Melly.
Gosh! I say, it does sound fun!

Everywhere a celebration,
Specially here on Wantage station.
  Bunting flying from the shops,
  Kiddies munching lollipops.
A cheer goes up thoughout the nation.

What's the reason for the party,
Why is everyone so hearty?
  All because I've made my ton,
  Me and dear Joan Hunter-Dunn!
I think I'll have another smarty!

(Not very good, is it? But put it in if you like. J.B.)

A podcast of this poem, read by Alan Bennett, can be downloaded from www.bbcbetjfest.co.uk

MING RESTORATION 'A TRIUMPH'

by Our Political Staff **Keith Vase**

A PRICELESS Ming party leader who was recently smashed into "ten thousand pieces" after winning the Lib Dem leadership election, has been painstakingly reassembled and put back on show in the House of Commons.

Said a party spokesman last night, "It is an amazing feat of the restorer's art. If you look closely, you can see the Ming is still hopelessly cracked, but from a distance one would almost think that he was as good as new (or rather old)."

Ming Campbell is 106.

Late News
KENNEDY DRIES UP IN DROUGHT

THE once fast-flowing Kennedy has been reduced to no more than a tiny trickle.

Where once vast volumes of liquid roared continuously down its throat, to the delight of journalists, nothing can now be seen but a parched and cracked throat.

"This is a sad day for all of us," said one Lib Dem MP last night. "We can only hope that one day soon we shall see the Kennedy once again brimming over, and ready to replace this hopeless old Chinaman that we made such a mistake by electing leader."

Charles Kennedy is 25.

BECKHAM
A Nation Mourns

by Our Football Staff **Jimmy Grieves**

THE GOVERNMENT is to declare a national day of mourning, following the announcement that David Beckham has been dropped from the England squad.

There will be a memorial service at Westminster Abbey to mark the death of David Beckham's career.

The Prime Minister, Mr Tony Blair, is expected to officiate at the service for the man he calls simply "The People's Player".

Sir Elton John will be performing a new version of his much-loved funerary anthem, *Candle In The Goal*.

The service will be sponsored by Gillette – the greatest shave a man can get. *(That's enough Beckham. Ed.)*

Late News – Fayed accuses Prince Philip of murdering David Beckham

CHATTO

"Far too many of these Asian fellows coming here, to my mind..."

"Still, if they're all like that chap Mahmood and the little Johnny with the turban..."

"... we can't have enough of them"

TERROR FLIGHT CHAOS

> I wish things would get back to normal

> Then we could be delayed by a strike

HOW TO SPOT A HOME-GROWN TERRORIST
Ten Tell-Tale Signs

1. Lovely boy
2. Plays cricket
3. Eats fish and chips
4. Keeps himself to himself
5. Grows long beard
6. Wears robes
7. Does chemistry degree
8. Visits Pakistan for long holiday
9. Very keen on the internet
10. Not very keen on the Jews
11. Turns shed into mosque
12. Obvious nutter

Exclusive to all tabloids

HALF-SISTER OF TERRORIST SUSPECT IS QUITE FRUITY

by Our Entire Staff **Phil Pageone**

IN A major breakthrough in the investigation into the plot to murder thousands of innocent British civilians, we can exclusively reveal that all the signs are there. In my expert opinion, there is a definite link between fruitiness and the girl in the picture.

A police spokesman from the Anti-Terror Unit added, "Cor! Blimey! Phwoarr! Look at those,

Sarge! Someone who is distantly related to one of the suspects is, in fact, quite fruity."

A top terrorism expert from the University of Birmingham said, "I can confirm that she really is quite fruity."

Said a spokesman for the newspaper industry, "This development came just in the nick of time. We were minutes away from printing a picture of a bald man with a beard, but luckily (cont. p. 94)

Full story & more pix: 4, 5, 6, 7, 8 and 94.

HAND LUGGAGE
Those New Guidelines

You will no longer be allowed to take the following items on board the aircraft as hand luggage:

- ☒ Bottle of water
- ☒ Baby's nappy
- ☒ Copy of Da Vinci Code
- ☒ Women's sanitary items
- ☒ Mars bar
- ☒ Trouser press (Corby)
- ☒ Whistling key ring
- ☒ Sellotape dispenser
- ☒ Upright piano
- ☒ Microwave oven
- ☒ Hearing aid
- ☒ Sudoku puzzle
- ☒ Dental floss
- ☒ Islamic terrorist
- ☒ Nuclear bomb

All these items must be placed in the hold.

"This is ludicrous"

NEW PRESCOTT SHOCK

MR JOHN PRESCOTT, the Deputy Prime Minister, stunned the world of politics last night by saying something sensible.

In a private meeting, Mr Prescott told shocked Labour MPs that President Bush's Middle East policy was "crap".

"We couldn't believe it," said one amazed backbencher. "Prescott said something that made sense, was factually correct and with which no one disagrees."

Mr Prescott's office was, however, quick to deny the allegations.

"It is extremely unlikely that Mr Prescott would have said anything so reasonable – and, besides, at the time of the alleged meeting he was busy groping his secretary on the croquet lawn."

LET'S MAKE MONEY

KEEP PROFITS FLYING!

MICHAEL O'LEARY SAYS:

Keep giving Ryanair money to send a message to the terrorists that no one is going to stop Ryanair cashing in. I promise that a million pounds will be flying one-way into my account.*

BOOK TODAY ON RYANAIR

the patriotic British Airline of Ireland (which was neutral during the Second World War but never mind let's wheel out Churchill again...)

*Flights do not include flights.

FREE with this week's Eye

The Wasps of Britain

The Wasps of Britain

A full-colour wall chart of the best-loved of British wasps.

ST CAKES CELEBRATES RECORD GCSE RESULTS

by Our Education Staff **Lunchtime O'Level**

THE PRESTIGIOUS Midlands independent £40,000-a-day boys public school today announced a record number of overall passes at GCSE.

Said the headmaster Mr R.G.J. Kipling "We are, of course, delighted. 110% of our pupils have got A* or better this year. I think this proves conclusively that our educational standards are higher than ever – as indeed are our fees."

Critics however, point to Kipling's controversial decision to allow pupils to opt for so called 'easy subjects' rather than the core disciplines. Kipling admitted that all of his GCSE candidates this year had only taken one subject – Wayne Rooney Studies.

Pass Poor

"WRS is one of the hardest subjects on the curriculum," he said. "Boys are required not only to fill in their names, showing their workings, but have to remember the pin number of their father's credit card. So much for being easy!"

Could YOU have passed GCSE Wayne Rooney Studies?

WRS GCSE Multiple-choice module

1. Is Wayne Rooney?
   a) A Manchester United striker?
   b) A spud-faced nipper?
   c) The boyfriend of lovely shopaholic Coleen?
   d) The author of 'Wayne Rooney – My life So Far'

Candidates should attempt only one question. Time allowed: 90 minutes

ON OTHER PAGES

Fruity girl at St Crumpet's gets 120 A*'s. Full story plus pics!

Am I holding it the right way up?

Let's NOT Parlez Franglais!

Lesson 94 Dans le Classroom

Teacher: Bonjour la classe.

Pupils: You what?

Teacher: Aujourd'hui nous allons learn to parler Francais.

Pupils: Leave it out! We're going to do media studies.

Teacher: Non! Non! Non! What about les langues modern – le French, le German, l'Italian? C'est important pour le future!

Pupils: Bollocks! Who needs French when everyone speaks English?

Teacher: OK, alors. Aujourd'hui we will learn to speak English.

Pupils: Fuck off!

93

The Labour Party An Apology

IN RECENT years we in the Labour Party may have given the impression that anyone who dared to mention the word 'immigration' in a political context was clearly a shameless racist, stirring up prejudice and emulating the worst excesses of the BNP. Official statements such as 'Howard Plays The Race Card', 'IDS Plays The Race Card', and 'Hague Plays The Race Card', may have led voters to think that the Tory Party were essentially a ruthless gang of extremist lunatics dancing round effigies of their spiritual leader Enoch Powell, while holding flaming torches and wearing pointy hats.

We now realise that there are far too many of these foreigners coming over here, taking our jobs, working hard and voting Conservative. Blimey, seen those Romanians, they're a dodgy lot. And those Bulgarians? They'd slit your throat as soon as look at you. As for the Turks, they're next, 90 million of them. And they're all Muslims. Where do you say you want to go? Chelsea Bridge is closed, Guv let's go that way.

© A. Cabbie, Minister for Immigration at the Home Office.

Letters *to the Editor*
Redefining Planetary Status

SIR – At last the International Astronomical Union have seen sense and decided to remove Pluto from our already crowded solar system.

Pluto was always the thin end of the wedge and had it been allowed to stay it would have opened the floodgates to all those other so-called Plutons.

Believe me, I have nothing against them but Ceres, Charon and the exotically named 2003UB313 have no place in our galaxy and will surely be happier remaining in their own solar system.

Mark my words, had Pluto been allowed to keep its official status it would not have been long before every "traveller" in the cosmos, every Tom, Dick and Harry X473, was seeking refuge here and we would have been swamped by dubious celestial objects including planetoids, asteroids and haemorrhoids.
Sir Herbert Gusset
The Old Observatory,
Jodrell Bank,
Barking

Tonight's Prom

Holst
"The Planets"
(minus Pluto)

"They're crying out for plumbers in Poland"

The Eye helps you decide
ARE YOU OBESE?
10 Tell-Tale Signs

- Huge bum
- Can't walk far
- Difficulty doing up trousers
- Can't see feet
- Addicted to cakes, sweets, crisps, burgers etc

- Sweaty face
- Broken bed
- Car won't go when you sit in it
- Er...
- That's it

BLAIR FLIES BACK TO IMMIGRATION CRISIS

We let anyone into Britain nowadays

HISTORIC MEETING

Which Spice Girl are you again?

NEW PERFUME LAUNCHED

Mmm... Old Spice

Does my bum look big in this?

It should do. You paid enough

11 ARRESTED IN TERROR SWOOP

by Our Cricket Staff **Christopher Martin-Jihad and Henry Blowup**

ELEVEN Pakistani-born cricketers were today being questioned by the ICC in relation to attempts to terrorise the English batsmen.

The suspects, some of whom were overheard plotting to destroy the opening partnership with a lethal mixture of leather and willow, have denied all charges.

But investigators claim to have solid evidence against the suspects, including a video of the leader, Inzamam al-Qaeda, volunteering to commit professional suicide by staying in the dressing room after the tea interval.

LATE SCORE: England 9 for 11

KATE & PETE WEDDING

"The bride and groom will now cut the coke"

GOVERNMENT PARDON FOR WARTIME 'COWARD'

BY OUR MILITARY STAFF **DAWN FIRING-SQUAD**

THE Government today finally agreed to award a long-awaited pardon to a man accused of "deserting his duty" in the Great War of 2003.

Tony Blair was at the time a young Prime Minister commanding the British Army when he refused to stand and fight George Bush over the invasion of Iraq.

"Yes, he was a coward," said Government officials. "But there were extenuating circumstances Tony was still shell-shocked from meeting someone as important as the President of the United States. As a result, he tragically obeyed orders and sent everybody else over the top to their death.

"However, now is the time for compassion," said the official. "We accept that Tony Blair was as much a victim of the war as those who died on the battlefield."

His supporters are now calling for a statue of the man once branded a "lily-livered traitor" to be erected in Whitehall with the inscription "He Lied For His Country" *(surely 'His Shame Liveth For Ever'? Ed.).*

Letters *to the Editor*

Not cricket

SIR – Contrary to the widespread claim that no Test Match has ever been forfeited before, might I refer your readers to the game played in 1911 between England and the Indian principality of Tikka Massala. Shortly after lunch on the second day, when the England score stood at 764 for 1, a number of man-eating tigers were released onto the field where they promptly consumed the two batsmen at the wicket, the Hon Frederick Canedish-Smythe and P.V.R.M. Steggles, the Warwickshire professional. The England captain, Lord Basingstoke, quite rightly refused to allow the match to continue until the two batsmen were given Christian burials. The umpire, His Royal Highness The Tandoori of Bhindi Gosht, was left with no choice but to declare that the England XI had forfeited the match. When it was later alleged by the family of P.V.R.M. Steggles that the tigers had been released onto the field of play on the personal orders of His Highness The Tandoori, the ensuing riots lasted for several weeks, resulting in the deaths of several million hapless Indians. If any of your readers would like a fuller account of this distressing incident, they will find it in my book *Black Day At Naipur* (privately printed, Toppo Press, £25.99).

The Late Sir Harry 'Toppo' Thompson
Cover Drive, Ruislip.

SIR – Not so much 'The Empire Strikes Back' as 'The Umpire Strikes Back'!
Mike Giggler
Via email.

The Guardian Friday September 1 2006

Letters and emails

Cricket and the Industrial/Military Complex

Dear Sir,
...er... er... the sight of a colonialist white umpire blatantly discriminating against a team of ethnic minority cricketers from the former subject peoples of the British Empire is a sickening and totally nauseating reminder that cricket is a direct legacy of the fascist, imperialist, elitist, sexist, homophobic, public school world... er... as I was saying, it was entirely sickening to my mind to see played out once again the only too predictable paradigm, as predicted by Karl Marx in his seminal pamphlet *Cricket As A Metaphor For Bourgeois Exploitation Of The Proletariat* (1849, now reissued by the Wheen Press).
Yours in comradeship,

D. Spart
14 The Old Squat, Tunbridge Wells.

Sir,
'Silly mid-on'? Surely 'silly umpire'?!

Mike Giggler
Via email.

Umpiring Made Simple

Six!

Four!

Out!

THE OVAL

Go home paying punters!

A ROYAL YEAR IN PICTURES